MEASURING THE ECONO

The Case of .

The scientific advances that underpin economi   health would not
be possible without research investments. Yet c   ng the impact of research
programs is a challenge, especially in areas that span disciplines and industrial sectors
and encompass both public and private sector activity. All areas of research are under
pressure to demonstrate benefits from federal funding of research. This exciting and
innovative study demonstrates new methods and tools to trace the impact of federal
research funding on the structure of research and the subsequent economic activities of
funded researchers. The case study is food safety research, which is critical to avoiding
outbreaks of disease. The authors make use of an extraordinary new data infrastructure
and apply new techniques in text analysis. Focusing on the impact of US federal food
safety research, this book develops vital data-intensive methodologies that have a real-
world application to many other scientific fields.

Kaye Husbands Fealing is Chair of the School of Public Policy at the Georgia Institute of
Technology in Atlanta, GA. She was inaugural director of the National Science Founda-
tion's Science of Science and Innovation Policy program and study director at the
National Academy of Sciences. She serves on the executive board of the American
Association for the Advancement of Science and is an elected distinguished AAAS Fellow.

Julia I. Lane is a professor at the New York University Wagner Graduate School of
Public Service and at the NYU Center for Urban Science and Progress, and a Provostial
Fellow for Innovation Analytics. She has published more than 70 articles in leading
economics journals, and authored or edited 10 books. She is an elected fellow of the
American Statistical Association, the International Statistical Institute, and the Ameri-
can Association for the Advancement of Science.

John L. King is an economist and researcher in innovation and science policy. During a
15-year career at the US Department of Agriculture Economic Research Service and Office of
the Chief Scientist, his research has examined intellectual property, industry structure, and
research impacts, in both the food and agriculture sector and more broadly. He is currently
Director of Analysis and Policy (Graduate Studies) at the University of California, Davis.

Stanley R. Johnson is Distinguished Professor of Economics–Emeritus at Iowa State
University, Ames, IA, and Assistant to the Dean for Special Projects in the College of
Agriculture, Biotechnology, and Natural Resources at the University of Nevada, Reno.
He also serves as Chair of the Board of Directors of the National Center for Food and
Agricultural Policy, Washington, DC.

Measuring the Economic Value of Research

The Case of Food Safety

Edited by

KAYE HUSBANDS FEALING

Georgia Institute of Technology

JULIA I. LANE

New York University

JOHN L. KING

University of California, Davis

STANLEY R. JOHNSON

University of Nevada, Reno

CAMBRIDGE
UNIVERSITY PRESS

CAMBRIDGE
UNIVERSITY PRESS

University Printing House, Cambridge CB2 8BS, United Kingdom

One Liberty Plaza, 20th Floor, New York, NY 10006, USA

477 Williamstown Road, Port Melbourne, VIC 3207, Australia

314–321, 3rd Floor, Plot 3, Splendor Forum, Jasola District Centre, New Delhi – 110025, India

79 Anson Road, #06–04/06, Singapore 079906

Cambridge University Press is part of the University of Cambridge.

It furthers the University's mission by disseminating knowledge in the pursuit of
education, learning, and research at the highest international levels of excellence.

www.cambridge.org
Information on this title: www.cambridge.org/9781107159693
DOI: 10.1017/9781316671788.

© Cambridge University Press 2018

First published 2018

Printed in the United Kingdom by Clays, St Ives plc.

A catalogue record for this publication is available from the British Library.

ISBN 978-1-107-15969-3 Hardback
ISBN 978-1-316-61241-5 Paperback

To John H. Marburger III

Contents

Figures

Figures

Tables

Contributors

Nathan Goldschlag is a senior economist at the Center for Economic Studies at the Census Bureau. He received his PhD from George Mason University. His research focuses on innovation, technological change, and business dynamism. He oversees a number of efforts to build new data resources by creating novel linkages between administrative and survey data.

Kaye Husbands Fealing is Chair of the School of Public Policy at the Georgia Institute of Technology, Atlanta, GA. She has served as inaugural director of the National Science Foundation's (NSF) Science of Science and Innovation Policy program; study director at the National Academy of Sciences; executive board member of the American Association for the Advancement of Science (AAAS); and committee member for American Economic Association, Council of Canadian Academies, National Academies, National Advisory General Medical Science Council, and NSF. She was elected AAAS Distinguished Fellow and has earned distinctions for outstanding teaching. She holds a PhD in economics from Harvard University.

Akina Ikudo is a doctoral student in economics at the University of California, Los Angeles (UCLA). She is a microeconomic theorist with research interests in mechanism design, game theory, and decision theory. Prior to joining UCLA, she was a modeling analyst at American Electric Power in Columbus, OH. She holds an MA in economics from UCLA and a BS in mathematics, an MAS in applied statistics, and an MS in industrial engineering from Ohio State University.

Lee-Ann Jaykus is an expert in microbiological food safety, with emphasis on food virology and microbial risk assessment. Her professional activities include the National Advisory Committee on Microbiological Criteria for Foods, various National Academy of Sciences panels, and the executive board (president, 2010–2011) of the International Association for Food Protection (IAFP). She is recipient of the North Carolina State University Alexander Quarles Holladay Medal for Excellence, IAFP Maurice Weber Laboratorian Award, and NSF Food Safety Leadership Award. Dr. Jaykus has taught food microbiology/safety for over 20 years, mentored 60 graduate students and postdocs, and authored more than 170 publications.

Stanley R. Johnson is Distinguished Professor of Economics–Emeritus at Iowa State University, Ames, IA, where he served as director of the Center for Agricultural and Rural Development (CARD) and Vice Provost for Extension. He has published widely in econometrics, food, and agricultural and environmental policy and advised hundreds of PhD students. He is a Fellow of the American Agricultural Economics Association (AAEA) and has earned numerous appointments to academies of science around the world, outstanding article awards, and Doctor Honoris Causa appointments. He chairs the Board of Directors of the National Center for Food and Agricultural Policy (NCFAP) in Washington, DC.

Yeong Jae Kim is a senior research associate at the Tyndall Center for Climate Change Research, Norwich, UK, whose research focuses on energy economics and innovation. He joined the Tyndall Center after completing his PhD at the School of Public Policy at Georgia Tech in 2017. As a graduate research assistant at Georgia Tech, he applied some of the quantitative methods he learned on how to use patent data in his dissertation. He is also a member of the Climate and Energy Policy Laboratory. He has an MS in agricultural economics from Texas A&M University and a BA from Hanyang University.

John L. King researches science policy and innovation. As an economist at the US Department of Agriculture (USDA) Economic Research Service and senior advisor/acting director in the Office of the Chief Scientist, he examined intellectual property, industry structure, and research impacts in food and agriculture. He participated in several Office of Science and Technology Policy initiatives to quantify impacts and enhance science policy, including STAR METRICS, the Science of Science Policy, and federal policy on open access to publications and data. Currently he is Graduate Studies Director of Analysis and Policy at the University of California, Davis. He received his PhD from Vanderbilt University.

Evgeny Klochikhin is senior data scientist and researcher with the American Institutes for Research, Washington, DC. He provides expertise to projects in several countries, with responsibilities including data collection, database development, and visualization. He contributes to the development of innovative methods of evidence-based policy and evaluation using advanced data science, computational techniques, text mining, and Big Data analysis. He co-leads the PatentsView project funded by the US Patent and Trademark Office. Dr. Klochikhin holds a PhD in public policy and management from the University of Manchester, UK, and has published in *Research Policy, Review of Policy Research*, and elsewhere.

Julia I. Lane is a professor at the New York University Wagner Graduate School of Public Service and at the NYU Center for Urban Science and Progress, and a Provostial Fellow for Innovation Analytics. She co-founded the UMETRICS and STAR METRICS programs at the National Science Foundation, and led the creation and permanent establishment of the Longitudinal Employer-Household Dynamics Program at the US Census Bureau. She has published more than 70 articles and authored or edited 10 books. She is an elected Fellow of the American Association for the Advancement of Science, Fellow of the American Statistical Association, and recipient of the Julius Shiskin and Roger Herriot awards.

Jason Owen-Smith is a sociologist who examines how science, commerce, and the law cohere and conflict in contemporary societies and economies. He works on projects that examine the dynamics of high-technology industries, the public value of the research university, and the network organization of surgical care. He is the Barger Leadership Institute Professor of Organizational Studies, Professor of sociology, Research Professor in the Institute for Social Research (ISR) Survey Research Center (CRC) at the University of Michigan, Ann Arbor, MI, and Executive Director of the Institute for Research on Innovation and Science (IRIS). He has received numerous awards for research and scholarship.

Matthew B. Ross is a postdoctoral scholar in the economics department at Ohio State University, Columbus, OH. His research uses tools from applied microeconomics and machine learning to investigate policy relevant questions from the fields of labor and public economics as well as the economics of innovation. He received his PhD in economics from the University of Connecticut.

Reza Sattari is a postdoctoral researcher in the department of economics at Ohio State University, Columbus, OH. He completed his PhD in economics at Simon Fraser University in Canada. His doctoral research evaluated the impact of various early childhood education policies on the development of cognitive and non-cognitive skills among young students. Reza is also affiliated with the Center for Education Research and Policy (CERP). He is generally interested in applying modern econometric methods and techniques to evaluate the effects of policy interventions in a variety of contexts that have direct implications for society.

Laurian Unnevehr is Professor Emerita in the Department of Agricultural and Consumer Economics at the University of Illinois. She has also held positions at the USDA's Economic Research Service, the International Food Policy Research Institute, and the International Rice Research Institute. She is a Fellow of the Agricultural and Applied Economics Association (AAEA), recognized for original contributions in the economics of food policy and demand. She received her PhD from the Food Research Institute, Stanford University, and her B.A. in economics from the University of California at Davis.

Bruce A. Weinberg is Professor of Economics and Public Administration at Ohio State University, Columbus, OH. His research spans the economics of creativity and innovation, determinants of youth outcomes and behavior, and technological change. He is an Institute for Labor (IZA) Research Fellow, National Bureau of Economic Research Research Associate, and associate editor of *Regional Science and Urban Economics* and the *New Palgrave Dictionary of Economics*. He has received support from the Federal Reserve Bank of Cleveland, the National Institutes of Health, the National Science Foundation, and the Kauffman, Sloan, and Templeton Foundations. He received his PhD from the University of Chicago.

Chia-Hsuan Yang is a research scientist at the New York University Center of Urban Science and Progress. She is an accomplished data scientist with expertise in research design, problem identification, econometrics, data analysis, record linkage, and machine learning. She has a PhD and MSc in engineering and public policy from Carnegie Mellon University and an MSc and BSc in computer science from National Tsing Hua University. Her research interests include economics of innovation, science and technology policy, and national innovation systems. Dr. Chia-Hsuan Yang has published articles on dormant IP licensing opportunities and impacts of offshoring on technology trajectories of global firms.

Nikolas Zolas is an economist with the Center for Economic Studies at the US Census Bureau. Nikolas started at the Census Bureau in 2012 after completing his PhD in economics from the University of California at Davis. Prior to receiving his PhD, he worked for UBS Investment Bank and started a non-profit corporation. Nikolas received his bachelor's degree from Rice University in 2003. Zolas's research interests are in innovation, technology transfer, intellectual property, and international trade. He has published papers in *Science*, *Research Policy*, and *World Economy*.

Foreword

The safety of food marketed to the public and promoting science for the public good have been concerns of local, state, and the federal government in the United States for a very long time. Safe food is essential to good health, as are clean air and water. The public cannot by sight, smell, or taste determine if food is safe, and unsafe food can spread disease and lead to debilitating illness and sometimes death. Hence, government has a role in assuring that food producers, processors, and retailers do what they can to deliver a safe product to consumers.

Creating the conditions conducive to science and economic growth was seen by the Founding Fathers as a role for the federal government. Its importance is underscored by its prominent placement in the US Constitution. Article 1 stipulates that Congress has the authority "to promote the Progress of Science and useful Arts, by securing for limited Times to Authors and Inventors the exclusive Right to their respective Writings and Discoveries." A century later as the United States was entering the Civil War, Congress enacted a series of laws to promote science. In 1862, Congress created the Department of Agriculture and assigned in the preamble of the Act "the general designs and duties of which shall be to acquire and to diffuse among the people of the United States useful information on subjects connected with agriculture in the most general and comprehensive sense of that word, and to procure, propagate, and distribute among the people new and valuable seeds and plants." That same year, Congress passed the Morrill Act, which established a Land Grant University in each state dedicated to "teach such branches of learning as are related to agriculture and the mechanic arts, in such manner as the legislatures of the States may respectively prescribe, in order to promote the liberal and practical education of the industrial classes in the several pursuits and professions in life." The following year, the National Academy of Sciences was created through an act of Congress to "whenever called upon by any department of the Government, investigate, examine, experiment, and report upon any subject of science or art." In its early years, the federal government repeatedly asked the new National Academy of Sciences to provide advice on food-related questions, especially ones related to weights and measures and how to determine the sugar composition of foods.

Fast forward to today, and both these topics – food safety and government's role in sponsoring scientific research – are still current concerns. There is a resurgent public interest in food safety. A foodborne outbreak of the past might have affected the attendees at the local church social, but today, due to the volume of production and rapid national and international distribution of food, a foodborne outbreak can affect hundreds or even thousands of people in multiple locations. Unlike measles, mumps, and other infectious diseases of childhood, there is no vaccine to protect a child from the common foodborne pathogenic bacteria and viruses. And the public is increasingly weighing in on concerns about other aspects of modern agriculture and the science of genetic engineering of food.

Public attention to accountability in government extends to the agencies that conduct and sponsor scientific research. Congress has stepped up its oversight of the science agencies through hearings and additional reporting requirements. Since passage of the Government Performance and Results Act of 1993 (GPRA), science agencies (along with all federal agencies) must set goals, measure results, and report annually on their progress. This scrutiny along with GPRA's legal requirements has led the federal science agencies to seek new ways to measure and evaluate the impact of their research programs on the economy, on health, and on other issues of public importance.

From the beginning, the science agencies struggled to find meaningful short-term and medium-term metrics for the impacts of their research investments that could be reported to Congress. The ways in which the scientific community evaluated research productivity – through numbers of publications, citation indexes, patents, awards, and other recognitions – met with little understanding in Congress and the public. Stories that related how research by multiple performers contributed to some public good were better received; for example, more milk is produced in the United States today with fewer cows than 40 years ago due to improved genetics, better nutrition, and advances in veterinary medicine, which can be attributed to a combination of specific breakthroughs from publicly and privately funded research.

In 2005, Dr. John Marburger III (who was then Science Advisor to President Bush) sought to bring research to bear on this problem and challenged the federal science agencies to develop a science of science policy. One result of his challenge was the establishment of a database of federally funded research grants called STAR METRICS (Science and Technology for America's Reinvestment: Measuring the Effect of Research on Innovation, Competitiveness and Science). When I joined the USDA as Chief Scientist in 2010, we were not yet contributors to this effort, but soon did join with NSF, NIH, and other federal science agencies.

Which leads us to this book. It explores the intersection of these two topics – food safety and accountability in science – and uses newly available data and new analytical techniques to provide insights into how the federal government's investment in food safety research is paying off. The research reported here would not have been possible without the work over the past decade on the science of science policy conducted by the science agencies and academic researchers, and I'm pleased to see that USDA's data coupled to NSF and NIH data provides the basis for this analysis of food safety research. The authors explore a variety of topics from the demographics of the food safety research workforce, to early career outcomes, patenting activity, and bibliometrics. The analytical approach illustrated here bodes well for the scientific community's future ability to communicate to the public the value of the research investment in food safety and other areas of science.

Catherine E. Woteki, PhD
Former Chief Scientist and Under Secretary
for Research, Education and Economics
US Department of Agriculture

Acknowledgments

This book both begins and ends with quotes from the late Jack Marburger, the father of the field of science of science policy. He provided the impetus for the establishment of the Science of Science and Innovation Policy (SciSIP) program at the National Science Foundation – Kaye Husbands Fealing was the inaugural program officer, and Julia I. Lane was the second. He also established the Interagency Working Group on Science of Science Policy on which Kaye Husbands Fealing, John L. King, and Julia I. Lane served. His vision, elucidated in many writings as well as the *Science of Science Policy Handbook* that was co-edited with Husbands Fealing and Lane, was that scientific empirical evidence, rather than advocacy, should be the basis for research investments.

The data infrastructure upon which much of this book is based is the result of much hard work by many people. The initial impetus was to respond to Office of Management and Budget and congressional imperatives to report the economic impact of the 2009 stimulus funding. The Federal Demonstration Partnership, under the leadership of Susan Sedwick, Cindy Hope, and Dick Seligman, supported both the development of the proof of concept pilot and the resulting program, STAR METRICS (Science and Technology for America's Reinvestment: Measuring the Effects of Research on Innovation, Competitiveness and Science). The federal support was provided by participants in the Interagency Working Group White House (Office of Science and Technology Policy), the National Science Foundation, the National Institutes of Health, the US Department of Agriculture, and the Environmental Protection Administration. The 2012 transfer of the program to a university-led activity was initiated by Roy Weiss at the University of Chicago and Barbara McFadden Allen at the Committee on Institutional Cooperation. The successful launch of UMETRICS (Universities Measuring the Effects of Research on

Innovation, Competitiveness and Science) was led by Jason Owen-Smith at the University of Michigan, Bruce Weinberg at Ohio State University, and Julia I. Lane at New York University, with the active help and support of Toby Smith from the American Association of Universities, Carol Whitacre of Ohio State University, and Jay Walsh at Northwestern University. The links to Census Bureau data were made possible by the vision of Ron Jarmin and Nancy Potok, to US Patent and Trademark Office data by Stuart Graham and Alan Marco. The links to dissertation data were generously provided by a license agreement with Proquest. Several program officers – notably Danny Goroff of the Alfred P. Sloan Foundation, Earnestine Psalmonds and Nimmi Kannakutty of the National Science Foundation, Robbin Shoemaker of the US Department of Agriculture, and E. J. Reedy of the Ewing Marion Kauffman Foundation – were critical to providing the initial grants that made the program possible.

We owe a great debt of gratitude to Sandra Hoffman, whose deep knowledge of food safety research provided invaluable guidance. She also greatly contributed to the organization of the expert workshop that brought together individuals with many different perspectives on the field. We also received excellent comments from three reviewers: Helen Jensen, Francesca Nelson, and Per Pinstrup Anderson. John Cuffe, of the US Census Bureau, also provided very thoughtful suggestions and input, as did participants at seminars at the American Association for Agricultural Economics and the Center for Economic Studies at the US Census Bureau. We thank Cameron Conrad, Ahmad Emad, Christina Jones, and Wei Cheng for research assistance; Greg Carr, Marietta Harrison, David Mayo, Mark Sweet, Jeff Van Horn, and Stephanie Willis for help with data issues; and Jay Walsh, Roy Weiss, and Carol Whitacre for their continuing support. Natsuko Nicholls at the Institute for Research on Innovation and Science, Nathan Ramsey at the US Census Bureau, and Craig Radford Schott at New York University provided amazing institutional help, and our very thoughtful editor, Teresa Barensfeld, was key to getting the document finalized.

Any opinions and conclusions expressed herein are those of the authors and do not necessarily represent the views of the US Census Bureau. All results have been reviewed to ensure that no confidential information is disclosed. This research was supported by USDA AFRI grant number 1005677; NSF SciSIP Awards 1064220 and 1262447; NSF Education and Human Resources DGE Awards 1348691, 1547507, 1348701, 1535399, 1535370; NSF NCSES award 1423706; NIHP01AG039347; and the Ewing Marion Kaufman and Alfred P. Sloan Foundations.

Introduction and Motivation

Kaye Husbands Fealing, Julia I. Lane, John L. King, and
Stanley R. Johnson

1.1 Overview

In the United States, improving the safety of the food supply has become a
national priority, and food safety research has been identified as central to
achieving that goal. Yet, little is known about answers to key questions,
such as: What research is already being done in the field? How many
researchers are active in food safety research? What are the characteristics
of those researchers? How do federal research funding patterns affect
current workforce development and future research capacity? What are
the reciprocal influences between food safety issues and federally funded
research? In short, what are the key ways in which federal investment in
food safety research funding will affect the research pipeline?

Of course, these questions are not unique to food safety research, but
this type of research is particularly interesting because of the diversity of
scientific fields and funding sources (including agricultural, health, and
veterinary) and the diversity of economic actors involved in agriculture,
food production, storage, and the movement of food safety risks across
domestic and international jurisdictions. Further, a continually evolving
dynamic relationship exists between private-sector agriculture (including
food production interests) and public-sector food safety research. To a
large degree, these are scientifically complementary, with each entity
exerting influence in the policy arena.

In addition, the importance of the field is undeniable. The Centers for
Disease Control and Prevention (CDC) estimates that more than 48 million
individuals in the United States alone – one in every six – will get sick from
a foodborne illness. Many of these foodborne illnesses will pass unacknow-
ledged as generalized discomfort. Many will be more severe, resulting in
lost time from work. Others will result in permanent disabilities or even

death. The CDC estimates that 128,000 cases of foodborne illness will require medical treatment and 3,000 individuals will die every year. The literature on the economic burden of foodborne illness is estimated as up to $77 billion annually (*1*). The US Department of Agriculture (USDA) estimates that just 15 pathogens account for more than $15 billion of economic burden from treatment, lost work, morbidity, and mortality, and this does not include other nonpathogenic sources of food safety risk such as food contaminants. Moreover, food safety is an issue of international scope: The total impact of foodborne illnesses is orders of magnitude higher than the effects in the United States alone, with incidence and impact higher in other countries and especially so throughout the developing world. In response to this, important policy changes have taken place in the field of food safety. Most significant is the legislation – the Food Safety Modernization Act of 2011 – which contains provisions designed to enhance the coordination of food safety research. Implementation of the act will affect long-standing research programs at federal laboratories, universities, hospitals, and other research institutions. Appendix 2.2 in Chapter 2 reviews the laws and regulations in the food safety industry.

A 2012 report published by the President's Council of Advisors on Science and Technology (PCAST) called for "creation of a new innovation ecosystem for agriculture that leverages the best from different parts of the broad US science and technology enterprise." In that report, PCAST recommended an annual increase in "investment" in agricultural research of $700 million, with suggested allocations to new graduate and postdoctoral fellowships ($180 million), new competitively funded research at the USDA's Agriculture and Food Research Institute (AFRI; $235 million), basic research at National Science Foundation (NSF; $130 million), and new private-public institutes ($150 million). The PCAST report is illuminating for two additional reasons. It notes that (1) mechanisms are needed for distributing funds to earn their highest return and (2) returns are not merely economic but also include the increase in human capital (or talent) developed as research is conducted. There is also an important role for food safety research because the sheer ubiquity of food consumption poses risks and creates opportunities for food safety science to reduce those risks.

Yet simply investing in research is not sufficient. The PCAST report highlighted lingering questions about the "appropriate allocation of research funds and whether they could be better spent on research challenges that are not a strong focus of the private sector" (p. 36). Of course, the lack of information about the impact of research is not confined to the field of food safety. In a speech titled "Why Policy Implementation Needs a

Science of Science Policy," John H. Marburger III voiced frustration that policymakers were not asking the right questions nor were they provided with sufficient evidence to formulate effective science policy. "How much should a nation spend on science? What kind of science? How much from private versus public sectors? Does demand for funding by potential science performers imply a shortage of funding or a surfeit of performers?" Marburger called for a new "science of science policy" to emerge, offering compelling guidance for policy decisions (2). He also noted that if there were to be better management of the national science and technology enterprise, then the practice of science policy must be professionalized.

Fortunately, that new "science of science" policy has emerged and is what forms the basis of the work in this book. That science is based on integrating new data on all steps of the research process, from the funding inputs to the outputs and consequences, by taking advantage of data from the federal statistical system. These new data, which are called the UMETRICS data (3), are what the authors build on in this book. This approach builds up from data at the level of individuals who conduct research – data that have broader economic and social impacts. The data provide answers to questions about the results of federal funding in the agricultural sector, particularly establishing mechanisms for assessing the impacts in food safety sectors. These are some of the key questions that must be answered for effective use of public resources to achieve food safety goals.

In sum, the work in this book seeks to answer some of the most important questions that are necessary to improve public policy about food safety research. This book describes new data and techniques that will enable, for the first time, a detailed examination of the outcomes of federally funded research in the agricultural sector generally and scientific outputs and outcomes related to food safety in particular. As such, this book provides a novel template that the science of science policy community can use to assess the impact and value of research that extends to other scientific fields. Of course, as with any research, much work remains to be done to characterize the full complexity of the impact of scientific research – and this book provides the first steps along a new pathway to do so.

1.2 Science of Science Policy: The Research Framing for This Book

A 2009 Pew Research Center Survey found that almost three-quarters of Americans agreed that government spending on basic scientific research, as well as on engineering and technology, "usually pays off in the long run." The same survey also found that roughly 60 percent of Americans said that "government investment in research is essential for scientific progress," while almost one-third said that "private investment will ensure that enough scientific progress is made, even without government investment." That year, private-sector firms and government agencies spent roughly 3 percent of total output in the United States on research and development (R&D). Federal expenditure on R&D was $133 billion, with about 25 percent of that spent on basic research. Almost half of the nondefense R&D budget went to basic research. Arguably, these expenditures advanced science, which in turn affected social outcomes, such as national security, health outcomes, food safety and security, energy and natural resource use, transportation, communication, and education.

However, estimates of the impact of science, technology, and innovation on society (from both the government and private sector) are typically based on multipliers and other proximate values. The calculation of economic returns, such as financial earnings from patent licenses, commercialized products, and spinoff companies, have typically been one-off approaches to assessing the benefit streams of expenditures on science. The calculation of scientific returns has often been based on counting the papers generated by researchers – a field known as *bibliometrics*. However, these measures suffer from several flaws. First, they do not strictly identify the outputs generated by any specific stream of funding. Second, the gross measures ignore the obvious necessary comparison: What is the additional output from these expenditures beyond what would have occurred given the status quo? Furthermore, these measures of outputs from research activities do not go far enough to measure the social impacts of research. The public wants to know how much their tax dollars contribute to improvements (or retrenchments) in social well-being. Assessing the public value of science and technology, therefore, is a critically important activity, because without such assessments, the collective citizenry would not be able to grasp the return on their "investments" in the scientific enterprise (4).

The lack of data on the impact of science expenditures has been a major impediment for some time for an informed decision-making process among both policymakers and legislators alike. Indeed, the 2008 White House Science of Science Policy Interagency Task Group undertook a literature review to determine the state of the science to date. The Task Group circulated a questionnaire to federal agencies to ascertain what methods are currently being used for programmatic investment decision making, as well as to ask what tools and resources federal agencies need that are currently unavailable. The Task Group found the following:

- A well-developed body of social science knowledge exists that could be readily applied to the study of science and innovation.
- Although many federal agencies have their own communities of practice, the collection and analysis of data about the science and scientific communities they support is heterogeneous and unsystematic.
- Agencies are using very different models, data, and tools to understand their investments in science and technology.
- The data infrastructure is inadequate for decision making. (5)

Historically, most of the estimates that were used for estimating the impact of science expenditures came from the Bureau of Economic Analysis's RIMS II model, which was derived from a decades-old input–output model of spending flows (and mostly uses national coefficients for industry or locally specific application). This approach also functionally equates the impact of science to the impact of building a football stadium or an airport: The impact is derived from the demand side and depends on the amount of spending on bricks and mortar and workers (6).

There are several challenges to building a better data infrastructure. The first is that the US scientific data infrastructure is oriented toward program administration rather than empirical analysis. The result is that the agencies primarily responsible for funding science operate in different data silos, with different identifiers, different reporting structures, and different sets of metrics (5). The second is that the focus of data collection is on awards, which are not the appropriate unit of behavioral analysis. Awards are the intervention of interest, and the activities of the scientists who receive the awards are what need to be followed. In other words, awards are temporal, but knowledge generation and resulting innovation require studying the activities of the objects of continuous analysis: scientists and their scientific interaction with other scientists. A third reason is that the current data infrastructure does not allow science expenditures to be coupled with scientific and economic outcomes. In particular, Grants.gov provides a unified portal to find and apply for federal government grants, but goes no further. Research.gov and Science.gov provide information about R&D results associated with specific grants, and a consortium of federal agencies provides R&D summaries (www.osti.gov/fedrnd). Another obvious challenge is the fact that the reporting system is manual (with obvious quality implications) and relies on principal investigators to make reports during the active period of the award – even though the impacts of science expenditures are often unknown until many years after the award has ended. Finally, despite the fact that funding agencies believe that their impact includes both workforce and social impacts, there is no systematic tracking of the students supported by federal funds. A previous effort to collect R&D information on federal awards, RADIUS, was discontinued in 2006.

The need to do better is compelling. There are continuing demands for evidence-based decision making on the part of research agencies, and agencies are eager to find methods that more accurately measure outcomes and impacts of their outlays (7). Traditional estimates are useful for comparative analyses, provided that counterfactuals are properly stated and measurable.

1.3 The Contribution of This Book

The goal of this book is to build a better understanding of how returns to research are generated, focusing mainly on data-intensive methodologies. As Daniel Kahneman has noted, the first big breakthrough in our understanding of the mechanism of association was an improvement in a method of measurement (8). The authors believe that this work will provide a new pathway for informing the link between research expenditures and research outcomes by building data at the most granular level possible: the project level.

This book builds on a vast literature on productivity growth and the social rate of return on expenditures on R&D in agriculture based on macro- or industry-level data. A number of important articles made great strides in using these more aggregated data to assess the economic returns to government expenditures: benefit-cost, risk and multiplier analyses, as well as econometric methods used to calculate multifactor productivity indexes (9–14). However, the resultant estimates of returns to research expenditures that use those techniques vary widely, particularly given the broad range of assumptions used to model relationships within the system. These measures are also highly aggregated, and they are most accurate for very near-term outputs from R&D expenditures. It is very difficult to quantify the longer-term impacts or spillover effects, at least partly because of the meso- or macro-level of the data analyzed.

This book's contribution provides a more granular approach. It exploits project-level data at a detailed temporal level to begin to describe *what* is funded, *who* is doing the research, and *what* the results are. At the heart of this methodology is the innovative UMETRICS approach of tracing research funding, which makes use of new computational tools to tie together disparate datasets (*15*). Chapter 3 spells out the approach in more detail; the approach uses natural language processing to describe (1) what research is being done, using proposal and award text to identify the research topics in a portfolio. Administrative records at universities and funding agencies describe (2) who is doing the research on federally supported grants on food safety and with whom. This is possible because of data drawn directly from payroll records, which also have the occupational classifications of each individual employed – including graduate students. This enables a characterization of the variety of occupational categories directly supported by agency funding. Finally, in response to the question of (3) what are the results, this research creates analytical links between researchers funded to do work on food safety and US Census Bureau data on earnings and employment outcomes. This approach represents a marked departure from the bulk of work seeking to quantify the results of research insofar as it focuses on the outcomes of the people who are involved in research projects as opposed to bibliometric method (i.e., counting the publications written).

Several methodological contributions go beyond the application of computational science to characterizing food safety research. One is that the approach focuses on the activities of not just principal investigators, but also the postdocs, graduate students, and undergraduate students working on food safety, as well as those working in related fields such as microbiology, zoology, epidemiology, and chemistry. This permits the construction of comparison groups. Another is the ability to construct direct measures of the way in which research funding supports research teams – this is particularly important given that science is increasingly being done by teams. A third contribution is the matches to outside datasets, which enable the capture of an important subset of the activities of researchers after the receipt of research funding – such as their PhD dissertations and their placement and outcomes. These sources are used to describe what results the funding has generated. Chapter 3 of this book describes the conceptual framework and data infrastructure used to assess the results of investments in food safety research.

1.4 Audience for the Book

There are multiple audiences for this study, both general and specific. First is the public. Federal research spending costs every man, woman, and child in the United States more than $200 a year. The returns to that spending are neither well documented nor well understood. This book shows how to trace the public value of investments in basic and applied research, with a particular focus on an area of great public interest – food safety. The second audience consists of funding agencies. The framework developed here should lead to a better understanding of the pathways to impact resulting from the investment of money in research. Third, university administrators can build on the data infrastructure at their own institutions to better understand the structure of research activities at their institutions. Fourth, researchers who work on science and innovation policy issues will benefit from the data infrastructure that has been created in the process of doing this study. The administrative records linked to Census data and to dissertation and patent databases should provide a fertile field for research in multiple areas.

In the specific area of food safety, policymakers in agricultural, science, and technology policy agencies should be able to benefit from the ways in which this study traces economic impact. The work provides new insights into the nature of food safety research, the composition of the existing and future workforce, and the pathways whereby food safety researchers connect to the larger economy.

1.5 The Plan of the Book

Chapters 1–3 introduce the conceptual premise of this book. Chapter 2 presents information about the nature of the food safety system in the United States as it is currently organized and regulated, which is quite complex, fragmented, and prone to obsolescence based on unanticipated events. It also provides a synthesis of the results of a workshop in which stakeholders from across the food safety research and food production chain provided input, and participants in that workshop produced two white papers. Chapter 3 describes the conceptual and empirical framework used for food safety research throughout the book.

Chapters 4 and 5 provide an in-depth discussion of new analytical and empirical techniques for describing research. Chapter 4 describes the fundamental step of identifying publicly funded food safety research from open records using computational techniques. Chapter 5 describes the structure of research funding in the sample of research institutions for which data exist, as well as the effects of different assumptions about food safety definitions on the scope of the research field.

The focus of this book then turns to an analysis of food safety research on the researchers and the research teams carrying it out. Chapter 6 begins by focusing on the individual researchers. It describes the way in which the data can be used to characterize who is doing food safety research, then matches these data to Census Bureau data to characterize the demographics of the food safety research workforce. Chapter 6 also describes how it is possible to use these new data to construct a control group of individuals that can be used as a comparison for investments in food safety research. Of course, since science is increasingly done in teams, one can also use the data to describe the structure of teams and their links to other areas of research; that is the focus of Chapter 7.

The book then turns to documenting the results of food safety research, using both traditional and nontraditional frameworks. Chapter 8 focuses on early career outcomes of graduate students and postdoctoral scholars who participate in federal research awards as part of their training. This analysis allows for employment and earnings effects of federal funding to be determined, compared with carefully constructed comparison groups. Chapters 9 and 10 examine patent and publication activity. While it is understood that patents are not a critical vehicle for the transfer of new knowledge in the food safety innovation ecosystem, the analysis in Chapter 9 does address the following questions: (1) What has happened to the pace and direction of patenting in the food safety sector? (2) What are the characteristics of US and foreign firms that are most active in food safety patenting? (3) What are the geographical and sectoral distributions of food safety patents? Chapter 10 follows with an analysis of scientific papers, which are an important source of policy governance. The methods employed in that chapter use new computational approaches designed to address two major weaknesses of traditional bibliometric analysis: (1) the limited coverage (and bias) of analyzed literature, due to the limitations of existing databases that tend to include a specific set of journals and subjects (interesting to their primary readership) and (2) the high cost of running a large-scale qualitative analysis of retrieved publications. Chapter 11 provides both a conclusion and a look forward to a future research agenda.

References

[1] R. L. Scharff, Economic Burden from Health Losses Due to Foodborne Illness in the United States. *J. Food Prot.* **75**, 123–131 (2012).

[2] J. H. Marburger, Wanted: Better Benchmarks. *Science (80-.)* **308**, 1087 (2005).

[3] J. Lane, J. Owen-Smith, R. Rosen, B. Weinberg, New Linked Data on Science Investments, the Scientific Workforce and the Economic and Scientific Results of Science. *Res. Pol.* **44** (9), 1659–1671 (2015).

[4]   K. Husbands Fealing, "Public Value of Science and Technology." Humphreys School of Public Affairs, University of Minnesota, Working paper (2012).

[5]   National Science and Technology Council, "The Science of Science Policy: A Federal Research Roadmap" (National Science and Technology Council, Science of Science Policy Interagency Task Group, Washington, DC, 2008).

[6]   J. Lane, Assessing the Impact of Science Funding. *Science (80-.)* **324**, 1273–1275 (2009).

[7]   K. Husbands Fealing, J. Lane, J. Marburger, S. Shipp, *The Handbook of Science of Science Policy* (Stanford University Press, 2011).

[8]   D. Kahneman, *Thinking Fast and Slow* (Farrar, Straus and Giroux, 2011).

[9]   Z. Griliches, Research Cost and Social Returns: Hybrid Corn and Related Innovations. *J. Polit. Econ.* **66**, 419–431 (1958).

[10]   Z. Griliches, Productivity, R&D, and the Data Constraint. *Am. Econ. Rev.* **84**, 347–374 (1994).

[11]   D. W. Jorgenson, F. M. Gollop, Productivity Growth in US Agriculture: A Postwar Perspective. *Am. J. Agric. Econ.* **74**, 745–750 (1992).

[12]   J. M. Alston, P. G. Pardey, Attribution and Other Problems in Assessing the Returns to Agricultural R&D. *Agric. Econ.* **25**, 141–152 (2001).

[13]   J. M. Alston, M. A. Andersen, J. S. James, P. G. Pardey, The Economic Returns to U.S. Public Agricultural Research. *Am. J. Agric. Econ.* **93**, 1257–1277 (2011).

[14]   J. Mullen, Productivity Growth and the Returns from Public Investment in R&D in Australian Broadacre Agriculture. *Aust. J. Agric. Resour. Econ.* **51**, 359–384 (2007).

[15]   I. Foster, R. Ghani, R. S. Jarmin, F. Kreuter, J. I. Lane, *Big Data and Social Science: A Practical Guide to Methods and Tools* (Taylor & Francis Group, 2016).

The Current Context

Kaye Husbands Fealing, Lee-Ann Jaykus, and Laurian Unnevehr

2.1 Overview

This chapter begins by defining food safety and food safety research, and then provides an overview of the ways in which such research has had an impact on food safety practices and policies. Much of this chapter draws from the input of a workshop on December 1, 2015, in Washington, DC, entitled "Assessing the Public Value of Government-Funded University-Based Research on Food Safety." The workshop was convened to engage the food safety and evaluation community in a discussion of the approach and key findings of the research. The workshop facilitated interdisciplinary discourse among researchers from a variety of academic disciplines and fields (e.g., food science, economics, and policy analysis), as well as communication and learning among academicians and policymakers. Participants addressed the following questions:

1. Data taxonomy: How should the scope of food safety research be defined?
2. Research sponsorship: How is food safety research funded? What is the role of federal funding and other food safety research funding? How successful have different funding strategies (big centers vs. many smaller teams or independent principal investigators) been?
3. Research inputs: Where is food safety research conducted? What is the demographic and educational composition of the food safety workforce?
4. Research outputs: What kinds of work activities are done in the first jobs of graduates trained in food safety? How do these early career activities relate to graduates' career paths? What is the role of food safety research funding in graduate student training?

5. Research outcomes: How does innovation occur in food safety? What are the economic impacts of food safety research funding on innovation? Are different kinds of innovation funded by federal and other funding sources? How does one think about the impacts of food safety research on the local, national, and global economy?

Workshop participants contributed brief white papers on the five elements in the preceding list, and Lee-Ann Jaykus and Laurian Unnevehr wrote two additional, extensive sections for this volume (Sections 2.4 and 2.5 of this chapter).

2.2 Defining Food Safety Research

Karen Hoelzer defined the scope of food safety research in a number of ways. In its broadest definition, food safety research should cover any research directly or tangentially relevant to food safety, for example, research in nutrition or food security, given that food safety is inextricably linked to both. The definition of food safety and its components must be reevaluated periodically, especially when new food production methods, research tools, or hazards come to light (1). Figure 2.1 provides a useful overview of the scope of the field.

Developing a comprehensive and consistent data taxonomy is imperative for the empirical research described in the later chapters of this book. Appendix 2.1 at the end of this chapter contains a compilation of definitions of scope provided by a selected number of peer-reviewed research journals with relevance for food safety, compiled by Hoelzer.

Scientific disciplines with relevance to food safety include, but are clearly not necessarily limited to: animal husbandry, bacteriology, biochemistry, biotechnology, chemistry, behavioral and cognitive science, communications, computer science, dairy science, dietetics, ecology biology, economics, education sciences (including adult learning), engineering, environmental sciences, epidemiology, evolutionary biology, food policy, food quality, food science, food technology, genetics (including phylogenetics), genomics and metagenomics, human medicine, immunology, law, machine learning, meat science, metabolomics, microbiology, nutritional sciences, operational research, parasitology, physics, physiology, poultry science, public health, public policy, risk assessment, risk communication, statistics, toxicology, veterinary medicine, virology, water treatment, and zoology.

Food Safety Research's Scope Spans the Complete Farm-to-Fork Chain

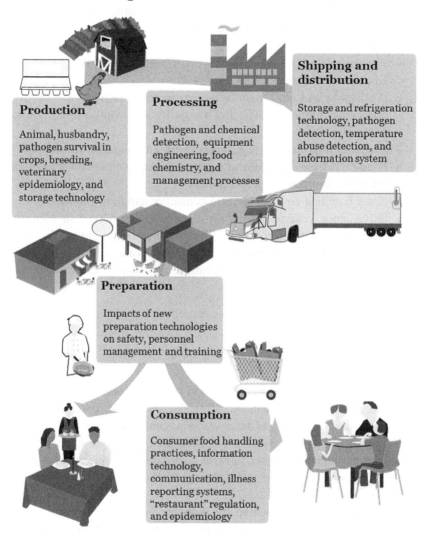

Production

Animal, husbandry, pathogen survival in crops, breeding, veterinary epidemiology, and storage technology

Processing

Pathogen and chemical detection, equipment engineering, food chemistry, and management processes

Shipping and distribution

Storage and refrigeration technology, pathogen detection, temperature abuse detection, and information system

Preparation

Impacts of new preparation technologies on safety, personnel management and training

Consumption

Consumer food handling practices, information technology, communication, illness reporting systems, "restaurant" regulation, and epidemiology

Figure 2.1. The scope of food safety research
Source: Centers for Disease Control and Prevention, 2010

The scope of food safety research spans the complete production chain, from the agricultural inputs used to produce the food or food ingredients (e.g., agrochemicals, animal feed, and irrigation water) to the timeframe during which foodborne illnesses are diagnosed and reported in surveillance systems. One way to organize this complex chain is as follows:

- Agricultural inputs, such as feed, agricultural water, manure and soil amendments, and others (e.g., vaccines, pesticides)
- Preharvest environmental factors, such as climate, soil, wildlife, naturally occurring toxins (e.g., aflatoxin), and others (e.g., flooding and drought events)
- Harvest-related factors, such as worker health and hygiene, machinery, and harvest technology
- Postharvest and food-manufacturing associated factors, such as processing techniques, storage, and transportation conditions (e.g., times and temperatures)
- Postharvest treatments (e.g., washes with antimicrobial substances)
- Food-processing conditions with opportunities for cross-contamination, microbial death, survival, and growth
- Retail handling and storage, and consumer handling and storage
- Surveillance systems, including diagnostic capabilities to identify, characterize, and trace back illnesses, foodborne outbreaks, and sporadic cases attributable to food (e.g., case-control or cohort studies); foodborne source attribution; and economics of foodborne illness.

Food safety research should consider one or more of the following aspects of the food system:

- The **food** itself, and how it is produced, stored, handled, and consumed
- The **environment** in which the food is grown, processed, and stored
- The **human** component, including the knowledge, perception, attitudes, and behaviors of food workers, consumers, and other stakeholders (e.g., medical doctors, nutritionists, and veterinarians)
- The **pathogens or other hazards** that can be associated with food, and their interactions with the food, the environment, and the consumers
- The **systems implemented by industry** to prevent contamination, outbreaks, or illnesses (e.g., Hazard Analysis and Critical Control Point [HACCP] system)
- The **regulatory and public health systems** in place to prevent, detect, or mitigate food safety issues (e.g., public health surveillance systems and regulatory oversight systems).

The breadth and diversity of food safety research clearly creates challenges for evaluating the efficacy of food safety research funding.

2.3 Food Safety Research Funding

Federal funding of nondefense discretionary research and development (R&D) in FY 2016 was $69 billion ($60 billion in 2010). Arguably, these expenditures advanced the science and affected social outcomes, including national security, health, food safety, energy and natural resource utilization, communication, education, and the development of the food system in general. Yet there is no consistent or systematic documentation of such outcomes from federal expenditures.

Specifically, for food safety, Table 2.1 shows that expenditures at the US Department of Agriculture (USDA), Food and Drug Administration (FDA), and National Institutes of Health (NIH)[1] totaled almost $2 billion in FY 2016.

FDA and NIH are agencies in the US Department of Health and Human Services (HHS). The FDA receives the largest share of non-nutrition-related food safety research funding. With almost $6 billion in program resources for food safety activities in FY 2015, the FDA received increased funding to bolster safety standards for domestic and imported foods under the Food Safety Modernization Act of 2011 (FSMA). The FDA's $301 million in increased funding for 2016 would

support mission-related research activities, including advancement of rapid detection and confirmatory methods for identifying microbial and chemical hazards in food and feed, as well as furthering partnerships with the Centers for Disease Control and Prevention (CDC), USDA, and NIH to evaluate and implement innovative technologies into FDA's compliance and surveillance programs (e.g., use of microbial whole genome sequencing). This also includes increasing collaborative efforts towards addressing antimicrobial resistance. The budget increases will allow FDA to focus on implementing FSMA and allow for continuation of mission critical research essential for supporting science-based food safety prevention standards, understanding and detecting foodborne hazards, and developing intervention strategies to protect the U.S. food supply and consumers. (2)

The USDA received $164 million in research funding during the same year. The USDA Agricultural Research Service (ARS) had an FY 2016 budget of $116 million, primarily targeting questions related to

---

[1] The USDA and HHS fund 90 percent of the nutrition-related research and training. The NIH is a key contributor to funding of nutrition-related research. Other federal agencies that contribute to nutrition research include the Department of Defense, the National Aeronautics and Space Administration, the Veterans Administration, the National Science Foundation, and the US Agency for International Development. Nutrition-related research is outside the scope of this book.

Table 2.1 *Food, Nutrition, Agriculture, and Natural Resources Sciences in the FY 2016 Budget*

	Budget Authority in $ million				
	FY 2014	FY 2015	**FY 2016**	Change FY 15–16	
	Actual	Estimate	**Budget**	Amount	Percent
US Department of Agriculture R&D					
NIFA[1]					
Food Safety	21	26	**46**	20	76.4
Food Security	37	40	**57**	17	41.3
Natural Resources[2]	19	19	**20**	1	3.3
Nutrition	127	123	**126**	3	2.4
Renewable Energy[3]	52	56	**50**	−6	−9.9
ARS					
Food Safety	112	112	**116**	4	3.6
Food Security	150	150	**163**	13	8.7
Natural Resources	201	201	**206**	5	2.5
Nutrition	87	87	**85**	−2	−2.3
Renewable Energy	32	33	**31**	−2	−6.1
ERS					
Food Safety	2	2	**2**	0	0.0
Food Security	4	4	**4**	0	0.0
Nutrition	16	20	**21**	1	5.0
Renewable Energy	2	2	**2**	0	0.0
US Department of Health and Human Services					
FDA					
Food Safety	1,218	1,229	**1,530**	301	24.5
NIH					
Food Safety	232	232	**233**	1	0.4
Nutrition	1,555	1,566	**1,600**	34	2.2
Nutrition – Obesity	857	857	**878**	21	2.5

Source: Agency budget justifications and other budget documents.

Note: All figures rounded to the nearest million. Changes calculated from unrounded numbers.

[1] Includes portion of Agriculture and Food Research Institute (AFRI) funding that supports education and extension.

[2] Includes soil and water conservation.

[3] Includes mandatory Farm Bill funding for Biomass Research and Development Initiative.

antimicrobial resistance in pathogens of humans and livestock and relationships among microbes and livestock, the environment, and human health. The questions were "designed to yield science-based knowledge on the safe production, storage, processing, and handling of plant and animal products, and on the detection and control of toxin producing and/or pathogenic bacteria and fungi, parasites, chemical contaminants, and plant toxins" (*2*). With an FY 2016 budget of $46 million, the USDA National Institute of Food and Agriculture (NIFA) focused its research portfolio on "minimizing antibiotic resistance transmission through the food chain and minimizing microbial food safety hazards of fresh and fresh-cut fruits and vegetables, expanding food safety education to new audiences, and pursuing new research strategies and technologies to create a healthier and higher quality food supply" (*2*). With $2 million, the USDA Economic Research Service (ERS) focuses on research analyzing "the economic incentives for food safety and provides a science-based approach to reducing food safety risks. This includes understanding the interrelated roles of policy and market incentives in enhancing food safety with a focus on the effects of the Food Safety Modernization Act (FSMA) on agriculture" (*2*).

As will become clearer in Section 2.4 on the food safety regulatory environment, the public benefits from "a modern, science-based food safety regulatory regime drawing on best practices of both USDA and FDA, with strong enforcement and recall mechanisms, expertise in risk assessment, and enforcement and research efforts across all food types based on scientifically supportable assessments of threats to public health" (*2*). This implies an imperative to link standards and policy decisions related to food safety to research, particularly research that is funded by several federal government agencies.

2.4 Food Safety Regulatory Environment

Food safety research operates within a highly regulated environment that encompasses the production, processing, transportation, and the wholesale and retail sectors (see Figure 2.1). It both informs and is informed by the current myriad of fragmented food safety regulations, which have caused inconsistent oversight, ineffective coordination, and inefficient use of available resources (US Government Accountability Office [GAO] Food Safety, main page) (*3*, *4*, pp. 17–18). Food safety and the quality of the US food supply are enforced by a highly complex system of laws that are administered by some 15 federal agencies (*4*).

The two primary US agencies are the USDA Food Safety and Inspection Service (USDA-FSIS), and the FDA, an agency within HHS. The USDA-FSIS is responsible for regulation on the safety of meats, poultry (and later catfish), both fresh and processed. USDA-FSIS also regulates processed eggs. The FDA is responsible for all other foods, both fresh and processed.

The other major players in federal food safety administration are the US Environmental Protection Agency (EPA), which is responsible for contamination by pesticides, and the HHS Centers for Disease Control and Prevention (CDC), which produce timely estimates of foodborne pathogens and illnesses and investigate outbreaks. Lesser players in the federal complex include the Department of Commerce National Marine Fisheries Service, the Alcohol and Tobacco Tax and Trade Bureau, the Department of Homeland Security, the Federal Trade Commission, and other agencies that are responsible for food security issues of a more limited scope.

The 2011 FSMA strengthened the food safety system and shifted the focus of the FDA and USDA-FSIS from regulations and responding by "containment" to "prevention" of food contamination and disease. The law had several provisions that require interagency collaboration on food safety, but the law does not apply to the federal food safety system as a whole (including other limited-scope federal and even state agencies). Thus, fragmentation in scope and content of regulations remains a continuing problem for federal and state agencies.

In 2015, President Obama advocated consolidating the food safety components of the USDA and FDA into a single agency responsible for food safety inspection, enforcement, and foodborne illness outbreak prevention and response. As indicated in the preceding paragraph, the emphasis would be on prevention rather than response to food safety emergencies. By the end of the Obama administration, this proposal was still awaiting consideration by Congress. While there has been major discussion for many years on such a coordination or consolidation, there is no indication that it will happen any time in the future.

Regulation exists at the federal, state, and even local levels, meaning that both foreign (imported) and domestic (locally produced) foods are subject to a very complex set of food safety regulations (5). One of the major requirements of the FSMA was the increased regulation of imported foreign food commodities. This resulted in at least twice the number of foreign facilities subject to FDA inspection between 2001 and 2011. Nevertheless, the FDA has not been able to fully achieve the FSMA-mandated level of inspection of these foreign entities, in part because of the need for substantial financial resources for implementation. The CDC monitors, investigates, and reports foodborne illnesses. It continues to claim that the United States has one of the safest food supplies in the world. Nevertheless, the *Salmonella* and *Campylobacter* pathogens alone account for about 2 million illnesses per year. On the domestic front, the USDA-FSIS (responsible for the safety of meat, poultry, poultry, egg products, and aquaculture products, as well as processed items from these foods) has also not achieved all its targets for pathogen control. Consumption of contaminated poultry products causes more deaths than the consumption of any other products (3). In February 2016, the USDA indicated that it is beginning to assess whether new pathogen reduction standard practices enacted in 2014 for eliminating *Salmonella* and *Campylobacter* have been successful in reducing associated morbidity and mortality. For detailed descriptions of federal food safety agencies, see Appendix 2.2 at the end of this chapter.

2.5 Food Safety Research and Training Landscape

Concerns about food safety have been with us from the beginning of human history. Well before people understood that microscopic organisms and invisible chemicals could cause disease, they were taking precautions to assure safe food and water, from cooking to fermentation to using copper containers for toting. Canning, for instance, dates back to the late eighteenth century during the Napoleonic wars, when it was developed for long-term food preservation at a time when refrigeration was unavailable. Louis Pasteur is credited with recognizing the role of microorganisms in the safety and quality of food – he invented pasteurization, although the process was not used to ensure the safety of cow's milk until the 1920s.

The first food safety regulations enacted in the United States were the Pure Food and Drug Act and the Federal Meat Inspection Act, both enacted in 1906. Prior to these, what few food safety activities performed were under the jurisdiction of the states. These acts basically forbade the interstate and foreign shipment of adulterated food. Changing the food safety authority from policing to regulatory, the Federal Food, Drug, and Cosmetic Act was passed in 1938. This act included recommendations for food safety standards and inspectional authority. All of these activities were initially under the jurisdiction of the USDA. However, in 1940, the FDA was moved out of the USDA, into what would eventually become HHS, essentially splitting regulation of our federal food safety system.

Since 1940, food production and processing in the United States has gradually moved from small, local businesses to large, diversified companies. This has resulted in changes in the organization of federal food safety oversight, as well as increases in federal regulatory authority in tandem with the private sector. For instance, the Wholesome Meat Act of 1967 and the Egg Products Inspection Act of 1970 increased USDA inspectional authority. In 1977, the meat, poultry, and egg inspectional programs were reorganized to form the USDA's Food Safety and Inspection Service (USDA-FSIS). In response to high-profile microbial outbreaks in 1996, USDA-FSIS launched its Pathogen Reduction/HACCP rule, which provides a prevention-focused approach to managing the safety of meat, poultry, fish, and egg products. Interestingly, the FDA and the products it regulates were not a part of these almost 60 years' worth of food safety regulatory developments, but that changed with passage of the 2011 Food Safety Modernization Act (FSMA). The FSMA gave the FDA new regulatory authorities and, like the HACCP rule, focuses on the prevention and reduction of microbial pathogens in foods. At the time of this writing, implementation of FSMA is under way.

2.5.1 Careers in Food Safety

Food safety is a scientific discipline dedicated to preventing the occurrence of unwanted negative consequences to human health due to the presence of biological, chemical, and physical hazards in foods. Because food can become contaminated with hazardous agents at any phase from production through consumption, food safety issues are relevant to the entire food chain and to all foods. Hence, food safety is an aspect of many different jobs within this "farm-to-fork" chain, which includes not only line food handlers, processors, and their managers, but also allied industries such as transportation services, packaging manufacturers, and vendors.

Those choosing to make food safety a career typically have advanced degrees (MS, PhD, or other professional degrees). Food safety employment is frequently subdivided by sector, that is, industry, government, academia, and nongovernmental organizations (NGOs). Table 2.2 provides information on how these sectors can be further subdivided and the types of jobs done by food safety professionals in each of these sectors. The table is comprehensive but not complete; there are about as many different food safety jobs as there are employers. All food safety careers require expertise in the food system and the means by which to keep it safe, but they usually require other skills as well, such as the ability to perform laboratory-based studies; management skills; and/or teaching, training, or instruction. While these jobs can be highly specialized (e.g., a bench-top researcher), many times they require a high level of conceptual thinking and the ability to see the big picture. Hence, breadth of training and expertise is key to success in these careers.

Table 2.2 *Sectors and Representative Jobs Undertaken by Food Safety Professionals with Advanced (MS and PhD) Degrees*

Sector	Subsector	Candidate Jobs
Academic	Teaching Extension/outreach Research Administrative	Professors (tenure and nontenure track), community college instructors, teachers, extension associates, postdoctoral research associates, and technical staff
Government	Research Regulatory	Bench-top researchers, research leaders, inspectors, outbreak investigators, regulatory affairs specialists, public health professionals, and congressional staffers
Industry	Food production Food manufacturing Food service Pharmaceutical Biotechnology Animal health Allied industries: • Sanitation and hygiene • Testing • Third party auditing • Packaging • Equipment manufacturers	Quality control/assurance managers, food safety managers, product development scientists, auditors, regulatory affairs managers, research specialists, process engineers, bioprocessing engineers, marketing, technical staff, medical doctors, and veterinarians
NGOs	Consulting Advocacy Trade associations	Consultants, risk analysts, statisticians, advocates, lobbyists, technical liaisons, and underserved populations

2.5.2 Graduate-Level Food Safety Training

Graduate-level food safety education (including MS, PhD, and postdoctoral training) has historically occurred under the auspices of food science departments or programs. With a few exceptions, these entities are located in land grant institutions with stated missions in research, teaching, and extension/outreach. Food science departments and programs are multidisciplinary in nature, and their faculties are frequently subdivided by either subdiscipline (e.g., food chemistry, microbiology, engineering/processing, and nutrition) or commodity expertise (e.g., dairy, meat/poultry, produce, fermented foods, and aseptically processed/packaged foods). While food safety usually falls in the food microbiology subdiscipline, it also includes food toxicology (chemistry) and bioprocessing (engineering) components. In fact, much of the research done in food science departments is applied and multidisciplinary in nature, involving two or more disciplines. For instance, food engineers frequently work with microbiologists, and nutritionists work with food chemists. Graduate (and undergraduate) students formally trained in food science receive a broad education in all of the subdisciplines and so are expected to have the capability to address food-system-level issues. A good example would be in product development, where the subdisciplines of food chemistry, microbiology, and processing technologies come together to create a safe and nutritious product that is produced in a cost-effective manner.

Food safety, as taught in food science programs, has traditionally focused almost exclusively on the postharvest phase of the food system, with an emphasis on food processing. By the mid-1990s, this model began to change, based on a general recognition that breaches to food safety can occur anywhere along the so-called farm-to-fork or gate-to-plate continuum. Consequently, food safety programs were faced with the need to address issues associated with the preharvest (animal and plant production, farming, harvest) and food storage and preparation (at retail, grocery, food service, and consumer) phases. By 2000, the public health community became more invested in foodborne disease, probably as a function of better diagnostic and epidemiological methods, as well as greater media coverage of foodborne disease outbreaks. This led to the implementation of the CDC's PulseNet and FoodNet. These are programs that are part of the CDC's surveillance system, allowing early identification and monitoring of outbreaks of foodborne illnesses.[2] In addition, the federal government began to embrace quantitative risk assessment as a basis for regulatory decision making and resolution of international trade disputes in food safety.

The end result was the recognition that food safety is a diverse field, encompassing many different disciplines. Those areas include, but are not

---

[2]   Founded in 1993, FoodNet is a program in the CDC's surveillance system. "By estimating the number of foodborne illnesses, monitoring changes in incidence over time, and attributing illnesses to specific foods and settings, FoodNet provides a foundation for food safety policy and prevention efforts in the United States." PulseNet is a national laboratory network run by the CDC, whereby public health and food regulatory agency laboratories are in communication around the United States. Since 1996, PulseNet has allowed "investigators to find the source, alert the public sooner, and identify gaps in our food safety systems that would not otherwise be recognized." Source: www.cdc.gov/ncezid/dfwed/keyprograms/surveillance.html (accessed May 2017).

restricted to, animal and poultry science, horticulture and plant pathology, communications and social science, laws and regulations, toxicology, mechanical and chemical engineering, environmental science, epidemiology, and biomathematics. A variety of colleges – such as colleges of agriculture, veterinary medicine, humanities and social sciences, engineering, and public health – teach these disciplines. Unfortunately, the academic model remains siloed, and graduate students are still trained in a single discipline, which frequently has core courses having little to do with food safety per se. Hence, at least in the classroom, these graduate students tend to be more narrowly trained and do not necessarily possess the breadth of expertise in the food system that is ultimately needed for their future professional lives. The take-home message here is that employers in industry and government need new professionals who are equipped with a breadth of training, ideally not at the expense of depth. This is not how the system currently works.

Historically, food safety–related research has been done in land grant institutions having a strong agricultural mission. The students trained in these institutions are at least exposed to agricultural issues and can speak that language. However, as the disciplinary breadth of food safety has expanded, some new professionals are training at institutions that have no formal programs in agriculture or affiliation with the foods sector. In this case, a dissertation topic may have a high degree of relevance to food safety (e.g., development of *Salmonella* biosensors or design of genetically engineered bacteriophage for biocontrol), but the student performing the research would know virtually nothing about the food production-processing-consumption continuum. The need to become experts in narrowly focused areas (their dissertation projects), and the tendency of institutions to stress research over classroom learning further restricts the opportunities for graduate students to become broadly trained. Of course, graduate training consists of more than just classroom learning; it also requires research and, in some cases, extension and outreach efforts. Herein lies the opportunity to build upon the depth of research training afforded in the classroom setting and to expand the breadth through extracurricular experience.

2.5.3 Changes in Food Safety Research Funding Landscape and Effects on Workforce Development

From 1994 to 2008, the National Research Initiative (NRI) of the USDA Cooperative State Research, Education, and Extension Service provided the pivotal program upon which academicians relied for food safety research funding. The NRI was reorganized in 2009 into the USDA National Institute of Food and Agriculture (NIFA), whose role is to support research, education, and extension programs of land grant institutions in an effort to advance agriculture and its societal impacts. Money to support this mission is provided as directed funds, formula funds, and competitive grants. Directed funding is driven by congressional special appropriations, which usually provide ongoing funding to a small number of academic institutions focusing on a specific issue; those funds are used in support of that initiative and stay with the home institution. Ongoing, state-appropriated formula funds support various functions in colleges of agriculture. For decades, a certain proportion of formula funds was released to departments to support graduate students and their research. Over the last 20 years and largely because of federal, state, and institutional budget cuts, most of these funds are now unavailable to support faculty-driven research efforts.

The Agriculture and Food Research Institute (AFRI) is the extramural granting program of NIFA (formerly the NRI). Funding is provided for research, extension, and "integrated" projects (those that cover two or three of the land grant missions); all can be used to support graduate student training. In part because of the transition from NRI to AFRI, it is difficult to track extramural agricultural research funding over the last decade. However, according to USDA-NIFA figures (https://nifa.usda.gov/data), the following trend has been reported for AFRI funding from 2010 through 2016: $131 million in 2010, $369 million in 2011, $183 million in 2012, $221 million in 2013, $258 million in 2014, and $278 million in 2015. These numbers include allocations for all AFRI programs, the Food Safety program being only a small part of that, likely less than 10 percent when considering the combined contributions of the Foundational and Challenge Area programs. Food safety funding can also be provided through other AFRI programs, including fellowship competitions, although these are not specifically designated for food safety work.

Other sources of funding are available to support food safety graduate research. Industry-supported centers (e.g., the Center for Aseptic Processing and Packaging Sciences, Dairy Foods Research Centers, and the Center for Food Safety) provide small amounts of money to multiple faculty members, usually within a single institution or a small group of institutions. Direct company-sponsored research has also been common practice. Some academic institutions have formal and informal partnerships with federal government agencies (e.g., the Institute for Food Safety and

Health, and the Center for Produce Safety) that provide funding and/or joint graduate-student mentoring. On occasion, federal funds are provided to a specific institution, on a competitive or noncompetitive basis, to address a specific targeted food safety issue. It is difficult to quantify the proportional amount of funding for graduate food safety research that arises from these various funding sources.

So, this is the current research funding landscape, but how has it changed over the last two decades? The general trends are twofold: (1) changes in the types of projects funded and (2) changes in the balance of the sources of funds. Both of these changes are driven by shifting priorities and dwindling resources. Industry-funded research has always been highly focused and results-driven. However, over the preceding decade the NRI program moved in that direction as well. Now, AFRI requests for applications (RFAs) are highly targeted, and submissions are not considered for funding unless they specifically address program priorities. In addition, there has been a trend away from small, less costly, single-investigator-driven work to larger, more expensive multidisciplinary projects. While having scientific advantages, this trend has effectively caused a decrease in the number of projects and a significant reduction in the number of investigators funded. The result: The money is spread over a smaller group of institutions, investigators, and food safety topics. The money is not going as far. Personal experience suggests that a good benchmark estimate is between $80,000 to $100,000 to support the work of one graduate student for one year, depending upon the institution and the project. It therefore costs as much as $200,000 to train an MS student and more than $300,000 for a PhD student.

These trends have significant impacts on young faculty career development. For junior faculty members, increased competition for research funds means more grant writing, especially because securing extramural funding is imperative for tenure and promotion. The push for research excellence can impede success in teaching or extension. There may actually be a disincentive for professors to engage in graduate student training, as postdocs are better prepared, more productive, and cost approximately the same as a PhD student, when taking into account stipend, fringe benefits, and tuition costs. Finally, with targeted RFAs, faculty research directions are much more prescriptive. This tends to squelch creativity and innovation. In other words, food safety research priorities set by agencies and industry are driving the intellectual direction of young faculty.

Many of the issues discussed in the preceding paragraphs have similar effects on graduate training. Students and postdocs, like faculty, are tied to specific projects with little flexibility to follow interesting tangents. Because funding is now so competitive, faculty can place additional pressure on students to "produce," sometimes at the expense of innovation and creativity. Although the research community has not necessarily observed this yet, it is quite possible that graduate student numbers will decrease as funding further tightens. Higher education institutions will be training fewer food safety professionals, or the ones being trained will have to be self-supporting. The increase in professional or nonthesis graduate programs and/or online programs may address the capacity problem, but likely at the expense of the rigor of training.

2.5.4 Demographics of Food Safety Research Trainees

It is difficult to ascertain the exact demographics for food safety graduate students and postdoctoral research associates, and those demographics are not likely to be uniform because of institutional and regional differences. Another major contributor to differences in gender, racial, and/or country of origin balance can be related to the advisors and their scientific expertise, ability to offer graduate student support (funding), and even mentor personally. Because of the highly dispersed and multidisciplinary nature of graduate-level food safety research, combined with institutional and regional differences, it is difficult to definitively qualify or quantify the demographics of the spectrum of graduate students in this field of study.

As might be expected, with increased attention to food safety and recognition of its interdisciplinary nature, there are many potential job opportunities for young professionals. So, which of the sectors described in Table 2.1 are graduate students and postdocs joining after completing their degrees? Unfortunately, because food safety is not a designated job category, it is extremely difficult to determine the proportion of young graduates who go into these specific sectors. The fact that food safety may be only one aspect of a particular job further complicates estimations. It is important to note that not all food safety trainees choose to stay in this field. Even those entering the academic sector may find themselves moving to nonfood safety areas due to changes in institutional mandates or funding opportunities, or to selection of collaborators. Therefore, the analysis in Chapter 6 of this book, on demographic characteristics, and in Chapter 8, on early career employment outcomes, is an important contribution to the literature on the composition of food safety sector human capital.

2.5.5 Meeting Stakeholder Needs in Food Safety Research Training

A central question for those working with future food safety professionals is whether their research training has satisfied both the demand and needs of future employers. The answer to this question may well be a function of the sector to which the trainee eventually aligns, and his or her specific job responsibilities in that sector. In short, it depends.

Performing research under the auspices of federal funding almost always relies on advanced scientific knowledge, usually focusing on the use of cutting-edge techniques and creative thought processes. This is particularly the case when training PhD students and postdocs. An unfortunate consequence of this is that the food safety or public health significance of the candidate's efforts may not be immediately evident or, for that matter, may never be recognized. In short, the research is "sexy" but may not be relevant to stakeholders. Students trained in this manner are best suited for academic or government research positions, where securing funds and producing advanced research is a prerequisite for success. Unless they have prior experience or are in an unusual sort of position, their research may not provide any real preparation for industry positions. Some companies may even complain that new graduates trained in this manner are poorly prepared for day-to-day problem solving because they do not understand the food safety continuum, are unable to address "big picture" problems, and lack the knowledge of and skills in management. In this case, one could say that the requirement for completion of a state-of-the-art research project and graduate degree may provide a launch pad into the workplace, but will also require subsequent diversification of knowledge and skills for a successful career trajectory.

Some graduate students complete research projects that are more applied in nature. These tend to be funded by industry and conducted by MS candidates. These students may learn techniques or answer questions that are more relevant to the industry, but they still may not be addressing specific industry needs upon joining the workforce. For industry in particular, graduating MS or PhD students may never actually use their research expertise while on the job. However, the basis of their decision-making responsibilities will need to be well grounded in the application of food safety principles.

Another important consideration is that, with the retirement of the baby boomer generation, employers are losing institutional memory in some of the foundational areas upon which food safety is based. Unfortunately, research in these areas (e.g., understanding and designing thermal inactivation strategies, sampling designs, or the evolution of food safety policy) is not funded by any source, meaning that academic programs are not always training new food safety professionals for relevance or for stakeholder needs. At this point, there does not seem to be a solution to this problem.

2.5.6 Food Safety Landscape

As is the case for so many applied fields, food safety education is at a crossroads. It is likely that the market for young food safety professionals will continue to expand, at least in part due to FSMA mandates. However, the ability to train graduate students and postdoctoral candidates using the traditional model may become increasingly difficult (because of dwindling funds) and may lose relevance (because of stakeholder needs). One view is that it is necessary to teach breadth and relevant critical thinking skills in food safety in order to prepare these young people for successful careers. This is not often accomplished in research endeavors, but can be addressed in coursework and/or by experiential learning, engagement in interdisciplinary research, and/or obtaining food safety certificates before graduation. While graduate-level research funding does have an impact on the qualifications of our future food safety workforce, it is only part of the larger picture.

Core food safety competencies have been identified in the context of structuring future undergraduate and graduate curriculum development (6). The approach taken was to identify and rank the relative importance of each core competency and identify the perceived knowledge/skills, strengths, and weaknesses. Both experts and new professionals were asked to rate either the relative importance (experienced professionals) or perceived knowledge/skills (young professionals). According to the experienced professionals, food microbiology, food manufacturing and processing, and risk analysis ranked as the top three competencies to be included in an undergraduate food safety degree program, with consumer, laws and regulations, and principles of public policy at the bottom. Young professionals considered themselves relatively incompetent in the following subdomains: risk analysis, surveillance and outbreak, principles of public health, laws and regulations, and principles of public policy. Figure 2.2 provides a visual summary of the rankings.

Johnston et al. (6) previously identified food safety core competencies, the purpose of which was to inform future undergraduate (and graduate) curriculum development. The group then prioritized the competencies based on the current needs of the workforce and compared those with

Competency ranking

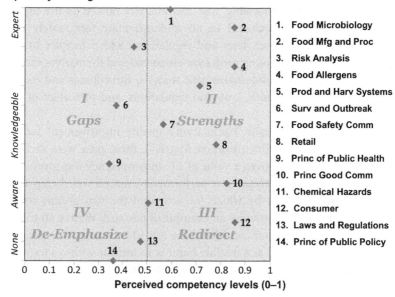

Figure 2.2 Competency prioritization matrix indicating results from competency ranking (y-axis) by food safety professionals and perceived competency levels (x-axis) among young professionals (scaled 0 to 1.0). Competency levels are based on binomial distribution (≤ 0.5 = incompetent; >0.5 = competent).
Source: Courtesy of Dr. Lynette Johnston of North Carolina State University.

the perceived competencies of new graduates. This was done by first collecting data on (1) expert ranking of the relative importance of each core competency ($n = 14$) as identified by experienced food safety professionals ($n = 25$) and (2) identification of perceived knowledge/skills strengths and weaknesses in the core competencies identified by a population of "new food scientists" (food science BS graduates with <5 years professional experience; $n = 114$). Both populations were asked to rate either the relative importance (experienced professionals) or perceived knowledge/skills (young professionals) using a rank from 1 to 4. A score of 1 indicated "None – very little knowledge of the topic"; a score of 2 indicated "Aware – limited ability to apply skill/knowledge"; a score of 3 indicated "Knowledgeable – ability to apply skill/knowledge"; and a score of 4 indicated "Expert – could teach to others." Results were dichotomized, representing a binomial distribution that defined competency as a score of 3 or 4 ("Knowledgeable" or "Expert") and incompetency a score of 1 or 2 ("None" or "Aware").

According to the experienced professionals, food microbiology, food manufacturing and processing, and risk analysis ranked as the top three competencies to be included in an undergraduate food safety degree program, with consumer, laws and regulations, and principles of public policy at the bottom. Young professionals considered themselves incompetent in the following subdomains: risk analysis, surveillance and outbreak, principles of public health, laws and regulations, and principles of public policy.

Using the Public Health Foundation's quality improvement tool (also known as the "3-Step Prioritization Matrix"), these data were dichotomized (competency was given a value of 1.0; incompetency was given a value of 0), and statistical analyses were performed. A matrix was then produced that provided a means by which the scores of the two groups could be correlated. Figure 2.2 provides an example of one such matrix. In this case, if an academic institution considered the top 10 core competencies identified by the stakeholders as a feasible number to include within a food safety curriculum, the four quadrants in the matrix provide information about how well the curriculum aligns with professional needs. The top right-hand part of the matrix ("Strengths") shows the competencies that are being adequately addressed in the academic program. The top left-hand section (quadrant I, "Gaps") includes several competencies that were highly ranked by the experienced food safety professionals: risk analysis, surveillance and outbreak investigation, and principles of public health. These are the areas that young professionals should be learning, even though they perceive that they have low competency in those areas. These areas should be better addressed when preparing young professionals for the food safety workforce. Quadrants III ("Redirect") and IV ("De-Emphasize") are areas in which institutions might either redirect their resources so as to fill the unmet educational gaps or completely abandon those teaching efforts. Methods such as these can help align curriculum development to be more consistent with workforce needs, resulting in better preparation of young professionals and greater satisfaction of employers with their training and performance.

2.6 Economic Outcomes of Food Safety Research

This section outlines the economic impacts of food safety research on society at a local and national level. It reviews the models and analytical approaches that are used to evaluate these impacts and the respective advantages and disadvantages of these approaches. Economic impacts are examined in three dimensions: market, health, and policy. This brief overview of research outcomes also provides some examples of the linkages between research outputs and economic outcomes. Given the wide range of potential food safety research, these are merely illustrative examples and cannot be all inclusive.

2.6.1 Improved Market Outcomes for Food Producers and Consumers

Improved food safety arising from food safety research can result in improved market outcomes or economic welfare gains, through shifts in supply, demand, or both. There are at least four pathways for such gains. In the first pathway, research may provide the means for firms and farms to reduce the costs of providing food safety. For example, research may develop new methods or technologies for preventing or removing contamination during any stage of food production from farm to table. By reducing the cost of providing safer food, industry can better meet private or public standards for food safety.

Industry and firm costs have been measured directly through survey data and estimated using production or profit functions (e.g., 7). An important consideration in such estimates is the distinction between fixed and variable costs. Food safety improvements have been found to have significant fixed costs, leading to economies of scale in the production of food safety (8). Thus, larger firms are typically better able to respond to new standards or demands for improved safety. This differential impact by firm size of new costs imposed by regulation is recognized as a more important market impact than any pass-through of costs to consumer prices, which is usually quite small at the market level (9).[3]

The second pathway for improved market outcomes is improved industry viability and reputation, and possibly expanded markets. Food safety incidents disrupt markets and can lead to loss of sales, reduction of firm

---

[3] The impacts of monopoly power in the food sector on consumer prices are a separate issue from the incidence of food safety costs and how those are distributed between producers and consumers. Food safety costs are usually a small percentage of final price, and thus they have very small impacts on consumer food prices. Therefore, most of the food safety literature has focused on differential impacts across firms. In general, there is little literature on the larger question of consumer prices and market power in the food sector beyond a few studies of the breakfast cereal sector. Most studies of market power in the agriculture and food sector have focused on the impacts of such power on prices that farmers receive.

equity, and even permanent declines in product consumption. More reliable food safety management can result from research that reduces uncertainty about food safety, which in turn allows firms or subsectors to maintain a reputation for reliable product quality, thus increasing market demand and improving the public health. For example, improved risk management techniques (or enhanced human capital to inform such management) may result from research and education activities.

Loss of market share, sales, and firm equity have all been studied through examination of the impact of specific food safety incidents. Widespread media attention to an outbreak typically leads to a reduction in sales and/or loss of market share for specific firms. For example, the 2005 *E. coli* outbreak in fresh spinach led to a loss of sales and consumers switching to other greens (*10*). Meat recalls have also led to a decline in stock equity (*11*). While the impacts of these outbreaks will often rebound, some economic disruption inevitably occurs across the supply chain.

Whether higher food standards result in a loss of sales or in a loss of market access has been explored in the international trade and development literature. New and more stringent food safety standards in high-income countries may have resulted in lost markets for developing countries. Wilson reviews the literature that shows that differences in food safety standards (sanitary and phytosanitary [SPS]) among countries reduces trade volumes and/or redirects trade among countries (*12*). This can also cause secondary and unintended consequences within exporting countries as food products that do not meet new SPS food safety standards are not exported and subsequently redirected into the indigenous food supply.

A related and third pathway for improved market outcomes is greater consumer confidence and product satisfaction, resulting in enhanced consumer utility. This can lead to increased consumption, increased willingness to pay, or both. Research can identify consumer demand for food safety and willingness to pay, which can inform policies and industry efforts. Consumer willingness to pay for food safety has been examined through surveys and experiments (*13*). These studies generally show a robust hypothetical willingness to pay for food safety. In a comparative study of willingness to pay for the same safety-enhanced product across valuation methods, Shogren et al. found that market behavior revealed the lowest demand for food safety, although all valuation methods provided similar results (*14*). This suggests that nonmarket valuations may somewhat overestimate potential market behavior.

Another pathway for improved market outcomes comprises reduced transaction costs in the certification of food safety, which can facilitate more efficient markets. Because food safety requires coordinated efforts throughout the entire supply chain, food safety management can fail when coordination is incomplete. When buyers along the supply chain can more easily identify risks and reward good food safety management from their suppliers, they can more easily ensure food safety for the final consumer. Research can facilitate better coordination through development of better diagnostics for hazards (e.g., rapid identification tests for pathogens).

Supply chain coordination issues, including those associated with the imposition of product traceability, have been explored through theoretical economic models. These models identify how coordination can be achieved at least cost with the most effective incentives for provision of safety (15). Case studies of particular supply chains have also revealed the specific mechanisms that are most effective in ensuring food safety compliance (e.g., 16), such as intensive farmer training and provision of credit to cover costs of compliance.

As demonstrated in the preceding discussion, the food safety economic literature is now quite extensive. As market impacts of food safety have assumed a higher profile in the past two decades. This literature has used different methods and approaches to answer questions of interest to policymakers and market stakeholders. The chapter now turns to public health and policy impacts, which can be subtler in terms of direct economic impact.

2.6.2 Improved Public Health Outcomes with Economic Consequences

Improved food safety can result in improved public health outcomes by reducing the incidence and severity of foodborne illness. This will have a positive economic impact through reducing the economic burden associated with medical costs and deaths arising from foodborne illness. Such improvements might be a reduction in acute illnesses associated with food intake (e.g., *Salmonella* infections) or a reduction in chronic health outcomes associated with exposure to hazards in foods (e.g., mycotoxins and liver cancer). The economic burden of foodborne illness includes direct medical costs of care, loss of productivity (i.e., missed days of work), as well as the loss in quality of life associated with premature death or severe disability (e.g., loss of kidney function from *E. coli* infection). A review of US estimates of the economic burden of foodborne illness is in *17*; these estimates range from $14.1 billion to $77.7 billion, depending on the number of pathogens covered and the disability-adjusted life years associated with each pathogen. These estimates demonstrate the economic significance of foodborne illness, but the wide variation shows that food safety professionals still have much to learn about this economic burden, in part because of uncertainty about illness incidence and severity.

Research can also improve the medical care associated with foodborne illness through a better understanding of illness etiology. For example, basic research in the virulence, incidence, and evolution of microbial pathogens has informed the care and treatment of illness arising from pathogens with shiga-producing toxins. It is now understood that such pathogens may lead to more severe complications or long-term sequelae. More effective diagnosis and care presumably lead to greater efficiency in the medical treatment of foodborne illness. This impact has not been directly measured.

Another important public health concern is maintaining the viability of antibiotics in health care. Routine subtherapeutic use of antibiotics in animal feeds has been linked to the more rapid emergence of antibiotic-resistant microbial pathogens and thus has been the focus of policy attention as a food safety hazard. Economic studies have examined the cost implications of reducing or eliminating subtherapeutic or even therapeutic uses of antibiotics in animal production (e.g., *18*).

2.6.3 Improved Food Safety Policy Outcomes with Economic Welfare Implications

Food safety policy improves when standards and requirements are based on a scientific understanding of foodborne hazards, their sources, consumer exposure, and effective controls. Such knowledge lays the foundation for policies that can focus on the most important public health risks and their prevention, thus most effectively using resources to improve public health (*19*). Food safety research has informed the changing focus of US food safety policy over time, as new hazards have been identified. The most well-established research relate to mycotoxins and pesticides and are grounded in toxicology models, which informed standards for the occurrence of these hazards and became established several decades ago. In the 1980s and 1990s, food safety professionals recognized the importance of microbial pathogens and emerging diseases such as bovine spongiform encephalopathy (BSE). New models and approaches grounded in risk analysis and prevention were developed or adapted to address these threats, primarily in animal products. The National Academy of Sciences issued three influential reports in the 1980s that informed the mid-1990s regulations for meat and poultry (e.g., *20*). In the 2000s, it became apparent that fresh produce could be an important source of foodborne illness, leading to new research on how microbial contamination occurs in these products and new standards for these products under FSMA. Research continues to play an important role in formulating new policies. For example, one support document for the final FSMA produce rule, "Final Qualitative Assessment of Risk to Public Health from On-Farm Contamination of Produce," had 237 scientific references, demonstrating the volume of research needed to develop this regulation.

Food safety policies can also be better designed to reduce the regulatory burden on industry and the costs ultimately borne by consumers. Furthermore, policies can be better targeted when there is an identified market failure in food safety. Private incentives for food safety exist, but they may be incomplete or fail to protect vulnerable consumers. Policies will be least burdensome when complementary to existing private efforts. Cost-benefit analysis of new regulations, including their distributional impacts on food firms and consumers, is a mandatory part of creating new regulations. Regulatory agencies also routinely consider whether the policy chosen achieves the public health goal with least burden. Such analysis is informed by economic research that measures costs, benefits, and incidence of burden, or identifies incentives for voluntary action by industry (e.g., *9* and *21*). Thus, food safety economics research can improve policy design and reduce regulatory burden, although such impacts may be difficult to identify in specific instances.

2.6.4 Concluding Remarks on Measuring Economic Impacts of Food Safety Research

It is clear that food safety has substantial economic importance for industry, consumers, and the general economy. And, as noted in the preceding paragraphs, economic research provides guidelines for firms, consumers, and policymakers, in addition to measuring the impact of food safety research advances in other disciplines. The discussion has referenced studies that use a wide range of economic models to understand the influence of improved food safety and food safety policy in markets and public health. These models draw on the entire field of microeconomics as well as selected areas of environmental and health economics. Any specific food safety research outcome will have particular real-world consequences, and thus the choice of economic methods or models for understanding impacts will vary accordingly. All of the approaches already mentioned can make important contributions to understanding food safety research and policy impacts.

2.7 Summary

Federal funding of food safety research is a public good. From farm to fork, the safety of the food supply is directly influenced by research outputs at universities that impact farmers, food manufacturers and distributors, the retail sector, the private sector and consumers. Best practices, standards, and certifications are all affected by food safety research done by food scientists and others representing myriad fields.

An important contributor to the development of new knowledge in the food safety sector consists of the students and other food safety professionals who are educated and trained in part through expenditures by federal agencies that support basic and applied research in several fields. This book uses analytical methods of estimating the impacts that these funds have on interdisciplinary research, graduation of students, and employment and earnings in food safety–related sectors. In addition, the book describes the linkages of such research outcomes on industry and the government sectors through patenting and publications in the food safety area. As will become evident in subsequent chapters, the public value of federal expenditures on food safety research should be assessed by looking not only at cost savings or other traditional economic impacts, but also at the development of human capital, which has complex and long-lasting contributions to the safety and security of the global food supply and socioeconomic welfare.

Appendix 2.1: Food Safety Scope

Table A2.1 *A Compilation of Definitions of Scope Provided by a Selected Number of Peer-Reviewed Research Journals with Relevance for Food Safety*

Journal Name	Scope	Reference
Journal of Food Safety	The *Journal of Food Safety* will not publish papers that Contain preliminary or confirmatory results. Come from meetings, workshops, or conferences. Evaluate the efficacy of bacteriocins, essential oils, or other antimicrobials, unless tested and validated in a food/beverage matrix. Testing in vitro will not be sufficient for publication. Focus on development of new microbial isolation or identification systems, unless tested and validated in a food/beverage matrix.	http://onlinelibrary.wiley.com/journal/10.1111/%28ISSN%291745–4565/homepage/ForAuthors.html
Journal of Food Protection	Major emphases of the *Journal of Food Protection* are placed on studies dealing with (1) causes (primarily microbial, microbially derived toxins, food-related toxicants, and allergens) and pre- and postharvest control of all forms of foodborne illness as well as risk assessment; (2) contaminants (e.g., feces, insects, rodents) and their control in raw foods and in foods during processing, distribution, preparation, and service to consumers; (3) causes of food spoilage and its control through processing; (4) food fermentations and food-related probiotics; and (5) microbiological food quality and methods to assay microbiological food quality.	www.foodprotection.org/upl/downloads/library/journal-of-food-protection-instructions-for-authors.pdf

(continued)

Table A2.1 (*continued*)

Journal Name	Scope	Reference
Food Research International	Topics covered by *Food Research International* include the following: Food chemistry Food microbiology and safety Food toxicology Materials science of foods Food engineering Physical properties of foods Sensory science Food quality Health and nutrition Food biophysics analysis of foods Food nanotechnology Emerging technologies Environmental and sustainability aspects of food processing Subjects that *will not* be considered for publication in *Food Research International*, and will be rejected as being outside of scope, include: Studies testing different formulations and ingredients leading to the choice of the best formulation or ingredient to be used in the manufacture of a specified food. Optimization studies aiming to determine processing conditions and/or raw materials that increase the yield of a production process or improve nutritional and sensorial qualities. Studies describing the production of ingredients and only their characterization without a strong mechanistic emphasis. Studies describing the antioxidant potential of foods lacking identification of the compounds responsible for the antioxidant activity will not be published. This is also valid for any other	www.journals .elsevier.com/food-research-international

Journal Name	Scope	Reference
	chemical compounds such as phytochemicals and minor components of foods.	
	Studies on antimicrobial compounds that do not consider a validation step in foods, lacking full data on chemical composition indicating the compounds responsible for the inhibitory activity and, when appropriate, the use of molecular biology approaches to support the findings.	
	Development of analytical methods not comprising a validation step in situ that represent the range of conditions faced during their application will not be considered.	
	Surveys of chemical, nutritional, physical, and microbiological hazards will not be considered. Only papers presenting a significant data set, wide coverage, novel and supported by adequate chemical or microbiological techniques will be considered.	
	Pharmacology and nutritional studies papers focusing in hosts rather than in foods or effects of processing in major and minor components of foods.	
	Pharmacology and nutritional studies that do not contain bioavailability or biofunctionality.	
	Engineering studies lacking of mathematical verification or validation in situ, when appropriate.	
	Fragmented studies, of low scientific quality, or poorly written.	
	Studies with no food component.	
Foodborne Pathogens and Disease	*Foodborne Pathogens and Disease* coverage includes the following: Agroterrorism Safety of organically grown and	www.liebertpub.com/ overview/ foodborne-

(*continued*)

Table A2.1 (*continued*)

Journal Name	Scope	Reference
	genetically modified foods	pathogens-and-
	Emerging pathogens	disease/108/
	Emergence of drug resistance	
	Methods and technology for rapid and accurate detection	
	Strategies to destroy or control foodborne pathogens	
	Novel strategies for the prevention and control of plant and animal diseases that impact food safety	
	Biosecurity issues and the implications of new regulatory guidelines	
	Impact of changing lifestyles and consumer demands on food safety	
Food Control	*Food Control* covers:	www.journals
	Microbial food safety and antimicrobial systems	.elsevier.com/food-control/
	Mycotoxins	
	Hazard analysis, HACCP and food safety objectives	
	Risk assessment, including microbial risk assessment	
	Quality assurance and control	
	Good manufacturing practices	
	Food process systems design and control	
	Food packaging	
	Rapid methods of analysis and detection, including sensor technology	
	Environmental control and safety	
	Codes of practice, legislation and international harmonization	
	Consumer issues	
	Education, training, and research needs.	
Food Microbiology	For *Food Microbiology*, following topics will be considered:	www.journals.elsevier.com/food-microbiology/
	Physiology, genetics, biochemistry, and behavior of microorganisms that are either used to make foods or that represent safety or quality problems	

Journal Name	Scope	Reference
	Effects of preservatives, processes, and packaging systems on the microbiology of foods	
	Methods for detection, identification, and enumeration of foodborne microorganisms or microbial toxins	
	Microbiology of food fermentations	
	Predictive microbiology	
	Microbial ecology of foods	
	Microbiological aspects of food safety	
	Microbiological aspects of food spoilage and quality	
Comprehensive Reviews in Food Science and Food Safety (CRFSFS)	*CRFSFS* publishes in-depth, extended reviews (more than 10,000 words in the body text and references) covering the chemistry, physics, engineering, microbiology, physiology, nutritional or sensory properties, analysis, risk analysis (assessment, management, communication), genetic modification, cost, government regulation, history, or psychological aspects of foods, food ingredients, food packaging, food processing/storage or food safety. Occasionally, special government and institutional reports are published, as well as symposium proceedings and reviews of books deemed to be comprehensive.	www.ift.org/ Knowledge-Center/ Read-IFT- Publications/ Journal-of-Food- Science/Authors- Corner/JFS-Aim- and-Scope.aspx
Journal of Food Science	The scope of topics covered in the *Journal of Food Science* include: Concise reviews and hypotheses in food science; Food chemistry; Food engineering and materials science; Food microbiology and safety; Sensory and food quality	www.ift.org/ Knowledge-Center/ Read-IFT- Publications/ Journal-of-Food- Science/Authors- Corner/JFS-Aim- and-Scope .aspx

(continued)

Table A2.1 (*continued*)

Journal Name	Scope	Reference
	Nanoscale food science, engineering, and technology	
	Health, nutrition, and food	
	Toxicology and chemical food safety	
Journal of Food Science Education	Appropriate topics in the *Journal of Food Science Education* include:	www.ift.org/ Knowledge-Center/ Read-IFT- Publications/ Journal-of-Food- Science/Authors- Corner/JFS-Aim- and-Scope.aspx
	Research in food science education	
	Results of original research involving new ideas, new educational tools, and/or novel approaches in food science education	
	Reviews	
	Recent important developments or trends in food science education	
	Innovative laboratory exercises and demonstrations. Innovative procedures in a format immediately useful to educators	
	Learning techniques and their assessment	
	New methods testing; distance and workplace education; curricular comparisons; cooperative and collaborative learning techniques; unique approaches to learning information; educational concepts; techniques for assessing curricular, professional, and interpersonal skills development; and similar topics	
	Book reviews on learning and educational developments as well as food science texts	
International Journal of Food Microbiology	The *International Journal of Food Microbiology* contains full-length original research papers, short communications, review articles, and book reviews in the fields of bacteriology, mycology, virology, parasitology, and immunology as they relate to the production, processing, service, and consumption of foods and beverages are welcomed. Within	www.journals.elsevier .com/international- journal-of-food- microbiology

Journal Name	Scope	Reference
	this scope, topics of specific interest include (1) incidence and types of food and beverage microorganisms, microbial interactions, microbial ecology of foods, intrinsic and extrinsic factors affecting microbial survival and growth in foods, and food spoilage; (2) microorganisms involved in food and beverage fermentations (including probiotics and starter cultures); (3) food safety, indices of the sanitary quality of foods, microbiological quality assurance, biocontrol, microbiological aspects of food preservation and novel preservation techniques, predictive microbiology and microbial risk assessment; (4) foodborne microorganisms of public health significance, and microbiological aspects of foodborne diseases of microbial origin; (5) methods for microbiological and immunological examinations of foods, as well as rapid, automated and molecular methods when validated in food systems; and (6) the biochemistry, physiology, and molecular biology of microorganisms as they directly relate to food spoilage, foodborne disease, and food fermentations. Papers that do not have a direct food or beverage connection will not be considered for publication. The following examples provide some guide as to the type of papers that will not be admitted to the formal review process. For a more extensive, list please refer to the journal's Guide for Authors:	

(*continued*)

Table A2.1 (*continued*)

Journal Name	Scope	Reference
	Studies in animal models that determine the responses of probiotic microorganisms in the gastrointestinal tract	
	Fundamental physiology and gene expression studies of food/beverage microorganisms, unless they directly relate to the food/beverage ecosystem	
	The isolation and characterization of antimicrobial substances such as essential oils, bacteriocins, etc., unless their efficacy is tested and validated in the food/beverage ecosystem	
	Development of new methods for the analysis of microorganisms, unless the method is tested and validated in the food/beverage ecosystem	
Food Protection Trends	The major emphases in *Food Protection Trends* include: News of activities and individuals in the field News of the Association affiliate groups and their members New product information Research reports as well as practical technical articles on food protection Excerpts of articles and information from other publications of interest to the readership	www.foodprotection .org/upl/downloads/ library/journal-of-food-protection-instructions-for-authors.pdf

Appendix 2.2: Laws and Regulations in the
Food Industry: A Review

This appendix provides a brief overview of US government and to an extent state legislation and implementation of food safety laws and regulations toward achieving food safety. The fragmented federal and state food safety laws have caused inconsistent oversight, ineffective coordination, and inefficient use of available resources (3, 22). Food safety and the quality of the US food supply is enforced by a highly complex system of laws and regulations that are administered by some 15 federal agencies (4). The two primary agencies for enforcement are the US Department of Agriculture's Food Safety and Inspection Service (USDA-FSIS) and the Department of Health and Human Services (HHS) Food and Drug Administration (FDA). The USDA-FSIS is responsible for meats, poultry, eggs, fresh and processed fish, as well as *Siluriformes* fish (e.g., catfish). The FDA is responsible for all other foods both fresh and processed.

The other major players in federal food safety administration are the Environmental Protection Agency (EPA), which is responsible for contamination by pesticides, and the HHS Centers for Disease Control and Prevention (CDC), which produces timely estimates of spoilage and foodborne pathogens and illnesses. Lesser players in the federal complex include the Department of Commerce's National Marine Fisheries Service, the Alcohol and Tobacco Tax and Trade Bureau, the Department of Homeland Security, the Federal Trade Commission, and other agencies that are responsible for food security issues of a more limited scope.

In January 2001, the Food Safety Modernization Act (FSMA) was passed by the Congress and signed into law by the president. This act strengthened the food safety system and shifted the focus of the FDA and USDA-FSIS from regulations and responding to containment to the prevention of food contamination. The law had several provisions that require interagency collaboration on food safety, but the law does not apply to the federal food safety system as a whole (including other limited-scope federal and even state agencies). Thus, fragmentation in the scope and content of regulations remains a continuing problem for federal and state agencies.

In 2015 President Obama advocated consolidating the food safety components of the USDA and FDA into a single agency responsible for food safety inspection, enforcement, and foodborne illness outbreak prevention and response. Again, the emphasis was on prevention rather than response or containment. This proposal is still awaiting consideration by Congress, and with the change in presidential administrations, it is not evident that this proposal will remain under consideration. It points to possible further coordination of the food safety programs of the two principal federal agencies (USDA and HHS) on both food spoilage and food pathogen regulations. Recall at this point that the food safety regulations cover a number of sectors: production, processing, transportation, and retail sectors. Figure 2.1, which is a diagram of the food supply chain from the CDC, provides a summary of these sectors and their responsibilities.

Imported products have been increasing and now account for approximately 15 percent of the domestic food supply. The United States is a net importer of foods (excluding agricultural commodities such as feed) with a net import balance of about $35 billion. The United States' main trading partners are Canada, Mexico, the European Union (EU), China, and Japan. Taste, price, healthiness, convenience, and sustainability of health conditions are the characteristics desired for foreign and domestic food choices. Regulation exists at the federal, state, and even local levels, meaning that foreign (and domestic) foods are subject to a very complex set of food safety regulations (23). One of the major requirements of the FSMA was the increased regulation of imported foreign food commodities. This resulted in at least twice the number of foreign facilities servicing the inspection of food over the decade to 2011. Nevertheless, the FDA (which handles this import function) has not fully achieved the FSMA-mandated level of inspection, detection, and dispensing other foreign food targets.

The CDC monitors and reports foodborne illnesses. It continues to claim that the United States has one of the safest food supplies in the world. Nevertheless, the *Salmonella* and *Campylobacter* pathogens alone account for about 2 million illnesses per year. On the domestic front, the USDA (responsible for the safety of meat, poultry, poultry, egg products, and catfish, as well as processed items from these foods) has also not achieved all the targets. Consumption of contaminated poultry products causes more deaths than the consumption of any other food products (3).

A2.2.1 Food and Drug Administration

The FDA has undertaken a number of steps toward implementing the provisions of the FSMA (24, 25). The set of objectives is comprehensive – relating to almost all FDA services, from detection, to improved identification of foodborne pathogens, to coordination with other federal agencies, to addressing prevention rather than monitoring, to working with consumer education as a way of limiting the contraction of foodborne illnesses. Subcategories for these objectives relate to specific aspects of the new scope of FDA of activities.

The FDA has published in the *Federal Register* proposed rules on third-party certification for imported foods and for those foods deemed to be at high risk according to the FDA. Some domestic companies have used third-party certification voluntarily. The FDA has proposed requiring all domestic companies to use third-party certification (*26*). This would continue the full change in the focus of regulation from containment to prevention.

A2.2.2 Centers for Disease Control and Prevention (CDC)

The particular branch of the FDA is CDC which CDC that works to protect the population of the United States and, in fact, populations from around the world, is the National Center for Emerging and Zoonotic Infectious Diseases (*27*). The CDC, FDA, and USDA-FSIS created the Interagency Food Safety Analytics Collaboration (IFSAC) in 2011. IFSAC represents a substantial effort to improve coordination of federal food safety responsibilities of the CDC, USDA-FSIS, and FDA. IFSAC was created, in part, in response to the key findings of the 2009 President's Food Safety Working Group (*28*). Specifically, in response to its charge, the IFSAC has set out specific objectives for interagency collaboration that cover the CDC, USDA-FSIS, and FDA.

The Surveillance Network (FoodNet) is a collaborative program of the CDC, 10 state health departments, the USDA-FSIS, and the FDA. FoodNet identifies the number of laboratory-confirmed infections caused by selected pathogens transmitted by foods, monitors changes in their incidence, collects information about the sources of infection, and disseminates information to provide a foundation for food safety policy and prevention efforts.

A2.2.3 Food Safety and Inspection Service

The USDA-FSIS is responsible for regulating and inspection of meat, poultry, eggs, and catfish, and all aspects of correctly packaged and labeled related products. Its strategic plan emphasizes science and education for those entering the workforce and is an example of the demand for graduates from universities and agencies with high-quality training (*29*).

A2.2.4 National Organic Program

The National Organic Program (NOP) was established by the Agricultural Marketing Service (AMS), an agency within the USDA to deal with the growing market share of organic producers, processors, distributors, and retail outlets in the United States. The NOP is different from other service agencies (e.g., FDA and USDA-FSIS) in that it employs private certifiers (contractors) to conduct most of its business. The certifiers are located in the United States and in foreign nations and are charged with qualifying organic producers and distributors for the processing, transport, wholesale, and retail for sale of organic products. In the United States there are 48 certifiers, and 32 certifiers (some from the 48) are based in foreign nations. Products coming into and produced in the United States must have an organic seal from the USDA. Certifiers must be accredited by the USDA, and training is offered for achieving certification. To keep current, the Organic INTEGRITY Database is maintained by the NOP to keep certification current for producers and others involved in the organic trade.

The NOP maintains a small group of "national food products certifiers" to check on the private sector certifiers. Organic producers and others are required to keep specific records on their operations and to have an inspection once per year. In addition, national NOP certifiers are permitted to carry out surprise inspections and to evaluate the quality of work of private-sector certifiers. The cost of certification is borne, except for the federal employees, by the organic producers and others in the food-marketing chain.

A2.2.5 Food Quality Protection Act of EPA

The Food Quality Protection Act of 1996 (FQPA) requires the EPA to ensure that all pesticides used for foods in the United States meet strong safety standards 30). The FQPA requires an explicit determination that the pesticides that are used for food are safe for children, and it includes an additional safety standard of up to a 10-fold margin to account for uncertainty related to children. The EPA regulation continues and foods are evaluated for safety every 15 years for chemical risks. In addition, the EPA also evaluates new and existing pesticides to ensure that they can be used with reasonable certainty and that no harm will come to infants and children as well as adults.

References

[1]   K. Hoelzer, How Should We Define the Scope of Food Safety Research? (2015). White paper presented at *Workshop in Assessing the Public Value of Government-Funded University-Based Research on Food Safety*, Washington, DC, December 1, 2015.

[2]   J. Zhang, S. Ohlhorst, "Food Safety and Nutrition in the FY 2016 Budget" (Washington, DC, 2016).

[3]   Government Accountability Office (GAO), Food Safety – High Risk Issue (2016).

[4]   M. T. Roberts, *Food Law in the United States* (Cambridge University Press, 2016).

[5]   S. Keenan, S. Spice, J. Cole, P. Banfi, "Food Safety Policy and Regulation in the United States" (2015), doi:10.1017/CBO9781107415324.004.

[6]   L. M. Johnston et al., Identification of Core Competencies for an Undergraduate Food Safety Curriculum Using a Modified Delphi Approach. *J. Food Sci. Educ.* **13**, 12–21 (2014).

[7]   M. Ollinger, D. Moore, The Direct and Indirect Costs of Food-Safety Regulation. *Rev. Agric. Econ.* **31**, 247–265 (2009).

[8]   L. Unnevehr, H. Jensen, Industry Cost to Make Food Safe: New and under a Risk-Based System, in *Toward Safer Food: Perspectives on Risk and Priority Setting*, Sandra A. Hoffmann and Michael R. Taylor, eds. (Resources for the Future, 2005).

[9]   S. Crutchfield, J. Buzby, T. Roberts, M. Ollinger, C. Lin, An Economic Assessment of Food Safety Regulations: The New Approach to Meat and Poultry Inspection. *Agric. Econ. Rep.* **755**, 1–19 (1997).

[10] C. Arnade, L. Calvin, F. Kuchler, Consumer Response to a Food Safety Shock: The 2006 Food-Borne Illness Outbreak of *E. coli* O157: H7 Linked to Spinach. *Appl. Econ. Perspect. Policy.* **31**, 734–750 (2009).

[11] M. R. Thomsen, A. M. Mckenzie, M. R. Thomsen, A. M. Mckenzie, Market Incentives for Safe Foods: An Examination of Shareholder Losses from Meat and Poultry Recalls. *Am. J. Agric. Econ.* **83**, 526–538 (2001).

[12] J. S. Wilson, Standards and Developing Country Exports: A Review of Selected Studies and Suggestions for Future Research. *J. Int. Agric. Trade Dev.* **4**, 35–45 (2007).

[13] J. A. Caswell, *Valuing Food Safety and Nutrition* (Westview Press, Boulder, CO, 2005).

[14] J. F. Shogren et al., Observed Choices for Food Safety in Retail, Survey, and Auction Markets. *Am. J. Agric. Econ.* **81**, 1192–1199 (1999).

[15] S. Pouliot, D. A. Sumner, Traceability, Liability, and Incentives for Food Safety and Quality. *Am. J. Agric. Econ.* **90**, 15–27 (2008).

[16] S. Kersting, M. Wollni, New Institutional Arrangements and Standard Adoption: Evidence from Small-Scale Fruit and Vegetable Farmers in Thailand. *Food Pol.* **37**, 452–462 (2012).

[17] S. Hoffmann, T. D. Anekwe, Making Sense of Recent Cost-of-Foodborne-Illness Estimates, EIB-118 (2013).

[18] D. J. Hayes, H. H. Jensen, *Brief. Pap. – Cent. Agric. Rural Dev. Iowa State Univ.*, in press.

[19] S. Hoffmann, Food Safety Policy, chapter 21 in *The Oxford Handbook of the Economics of Food Consumption and Policy* (Oxford University Press, 2011).

[20] National Research Council, *Meat and Poultry Inspection: The Scientific Basis of the Nation's Program* (National Academy Press, Washington DC, 1985).

[21] K. Segerson, Mandatory versus Voluntary Approaches to Food Safety. *Agribusiness*. **15**, 53–70 (1999).

[22] Government Accountability Office (GAO), "A National Strategy Is Needed to Address Fragmentation in Federal Oversight" (2017).

[23] European Parliament, Directorate-General for International Policies "Food Safety and Regulation in the United States" (2015) available at www.europarl.europa.eu/RegData/etudes/STUD/2015/536324/IPOL_STU(2015)536324_EN.pdf.

[24] Food and Drug Administration, "Operational Strategy for Implementing the FDA Food Safety Modernization Act (FSMA)" (2014), available at www.fda.gov/Food/GuidanceRegulation/FSMA/ucm395105.htm.

[25] Food and Drug Administration, "Strategic Plan for Regulatory Science," available at www.fda.gov/ScienceResearch/SpecialTopics/RegulatoryScience/ucm267719.htm.

[26] Hogan Lovells, "FDA Releases FSMA Final Rule on Accreditation of Third Party Certification Bodies" (2016), available at www.gmaonline.org/file-manager/HL Memo – FDA Releases FSMA Final Rule on Accreditation of Third Party Certification Bodies (2).PDF.

[27] Center for Disease Control and Prevention, "FoodNet 2014 Annual Foodborne Illness Surveillance Report" (2016a) available at www.cdc.gov/foodnet/reports/annual-reports-2014.

[28] The White House, "The Federal Food Safety Working Group Progress Report" (Washington, DC, 2011), available at https://obamawhitehouse.archives.gov/sites/default/files/fswg_report_final.pdf.

[29] Food Safety and Inspection Service, "Strategic Plan 2011–2016," available at www.fsis.usda.gov/shared/PDF/Strategic_Plan_2011-2016.pdf.

[30] US Environmental Protection Agency (USEPA), "Food Quality Protection Act (FQPA)" (2016) available at www.epa.gov/safepestcontrol.

3

The Conceptual and Empirical Framework

Nathan Goldschlag, Julia I. Lane, Bruce Weinberg, and Nikolas Zolas

3.1 Introduction

The goal of this book is to build a better understanding of how returns to research are generated. That understanding is facilitated here by creating explicit linkages between what is funded, who is funded, and the results. This chapter spells out the conceptual and empirical basis of the approach on which the book is grounded and provides a roadmap to the rest of the book.

The core insight that drives our approach is importance of the people – students, principal investigators, postdoctoral researchers, and research staff – who conduct research, create new knowledge, and transmit that knowledge into the broader economy (1). Much has been made of the role of documents – like papers and patents – but this chapter instead builds on Oppenheimer's insight that the best way to send knowledge is to wrap it up in a person (2). Indeed, the regional economic activity surrounding universities strongly suggests that regionally bound human beings, not globally accessible documents, are the key to understanding economic impact.

The conceptual framework is straightforward. Undergraduate students, graduate students, and postdoctoral fellows employed as part of scientific projects obtain valuable training while at the same time creating new knowledge that can be transmitted to their employers once their training is complete. The gains that result from the application of knowledge acquired through research and training accrue to both the employing firm and the workers. Researchers create new ideas that either directly generate new businesses or are transmitted through social and scientific networks to the private sector. Propinquity is a major driver of these effects (3).

The empirical framework mirrors the conceptual framework. It uses university data on grant expenditures to characterize who is working on which grants, then traces their subsequent activity through matches with administrative data from the universities, US Census Bureau and other sources.

This approach permits new insights into the impact of science. The size of the dataset is large enough to examine outcomes of quite narrowly defined fields, such as food safety research, or different demographic groups. The link to Census Bureau data opens a whole host of possibilities. With these data, one can describe the arc of a scientific career or trace economic impact over time and on an ongoing basis. It is now possible to describe real economic impact, because identifying comparison groups has become feasible. While the data platform UMETRICS make it possible to describe some of the networks resulting from grants, the match to Census data enables us to trace the subsequent dynamics in terms of the flows of those researchers to businesses and even to start-ups (UMETRICS stands for Universities: Measuring the Impacts of Research on Innovation, Competitiveness, and Science; see http://iris.isr.umich.edu).

3.2 A Conceptual Framework

At the heart of our approach is the recognition that the core outcome of interest for science funders is the creation, transmission, and adoption of scientific ideas. These ideas are generated within social (both scientific and economic) networks. Science funding works in part by enabling those networks to exist and expand.

Here, the theory of change is that there is a link between funding and the way in which those networks assemble. There is, in turn, a link between research networks and the way in which ideas are created and transmitted – and hence generate scientific, social, economic, and workforce "products." Of course, these causal links are often long and tenuous, and this book describes just the first steps in capturing the links (4).

The following two econometric relations (more, precisely, two groups of interrelated regression equations) illustrate the approach more formally: [1]

$$(1) \ Y_{it}^{(1)} = Y_{it}^{(2)}\alpha + X_{it}^{(1)}\lambda + \varepsilon_{it} \ \text{and} \ (2) \ Y_{it}^{(2)} = Z_{it}\beta + X_{it}^{(2)}\mu + \eta_{it},$$

where the subscripts i and t denote individuals and time, respectively. $Y^{(1)}$ is the output variable: the creation, transmission, and adoption of ideas. $Y^{(2)}$ is the network structure. Both variables are determined by a set of control variables $X^{(1)}$ and $X^{(2)}$ that can overlap, such as scientific

[1]   This specification draws on joint work of Lane with Jacques Mairesse and Paula Stephan.

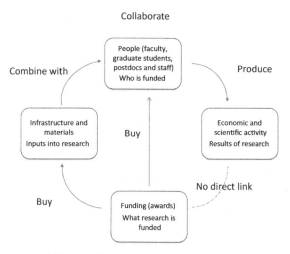

Figure 3.1. Conceptual framework

infrastructure or the prior state of knowledge. The variable of key interest, Z, is research funding for food safety. The parameters of interest include α, the efficiency with which research networks convert their activities into the transmission and adoption of ideas, and β, the efficiency whereby funding creates and sustains those networks. The remaining parameters, λ and μ, reflect the importance of the contribution of the control factors; ε and η stand for unobserved factors, including pure serendipity, and errors of measurement and specification.

Figure 3.1 provides a graphical view in which individual researchers (or, more generally, the research community consisting of networks of researchers) are identified as the "engine" that generates ideas.

This chapter describes the empirical counterpart to the conceptual framework. The funding inputs (what is funded) are connected to researchers and their scientific networks (who is funded). These in turn are connected to their subsequent activities (the results) in terms of the traditional outcomes of publications and patents, as well as the earnings and employment outcomes of trained researchers and business start-ups.

3.3 Previous Work

The core questions to be answered in managing any set of research investments, including the field of food safety, are: What is funded, who is funded, and what are the results?

There is limited information on *what* research is funded by the federal government, as a report by the National Research Council shows:

Two surveys ... provide some of the most significant data available to understand research and development (R&D) spending and policy in the United States. **Budget officials at science agencies, Congress, and interest groups representing scientists, engineers, and high technology industries, among others, constantly cite the survey results – or studies based on those results – in making public policy arguments**. However, the survey data are of insufficient quality and timeliness to support many of the demands put on them ... **The information provided to SRS [Science Resource Statistics] is often a rough estimate, frequently based on unexamined assumptions that originated years earlier**. (National Research Council 2010, p. 1, emphases added) *(5)*

Some administrative data are available. The research.gov website od rgw National Science Foundation (NSF) (www.research.gov) and the National Institutes of Health (NIH) *RePORTER* (http://projectreporter.nih.gov/reporter.cfm) are very useful tools for capturing information about individual awards, but do not provide a good overview of the funding landscape.

In the specific case of food safety research, as Chapter 2 suggests, there is a great deal of uncertainty about how much research is being done. Chapter 4 will describe how text analysis of grant abstracts and dissertations can be used to develop a better understanding of the funding allocated to a field of research.

Some research has been done on the question of *who* has been funded *(6, 7)*. But, as Freeman points out, the data are quite limited – in fact, there are more data on agricultural produce than on the science and engineering workforce *(8)*. Chapter 5 will describe in more detail the contributions of a wide variety of individuals funded by research, including faculty, graduate students, and postdoctoral fellows.

There is some evidence on the *results* of research, which are wide-ranging and complex. At the aggregate level, serious academic work suggests that the private returns to R&D investment in firms average around 20–30 percent, and the social returns roughly twice that. Other work attributes much of productivity growth in the 1990s to investments in information technology, which were driven at least partly by investments in basic research. Some work has been done analyzing patent clusters *(9, 10)*, and the geographic and industry placement of new PhDs *(11, 12, 13)*. However, as Reedy et al. point out,

Historically, progress in science and engineering has been measured largely by its inputs, such as the amount of dollars devoted to research and development or the number of engineers educated at our universities. Outputs, such as the number of new inventions or new businesses started each year, may be more difficult to measure, but they also give us a better sense of our economic impact in these arenas. Given the significant resources devoted to science and engineering, more attention to this type of metric is long overdue. (*14*)

Although it would be impossible to capture all results, a major contribution of our work is the systematic description of some of the multiple ways in which scientific ideas about food safety are transmitted to the broader economy. Some of them are in written form – publications, patents, and PhD dissertations. Importantly, however, this book describes how ideas are transmitted through the employment placement of people trained in food safety research and reports on their subsequent employment outcomes.

3.4 Empirical Framework

The work in this book draws on recent large-scale investments to build administrative data that cover researchers supported by both federal and nonfederal grants in a subset of major universities participating in the UMETRICS project (*15*). Data on the full team of researchers supported on each research grant for each payroll period are captured; they are drawn directly from payroll records. These data have been linked to Census Bureau data, to connect people to *all* their subsequent jobs and employers in the United States[2]

This connection is possible because the universities have provided identifiers that allow researchers, under strict confidentiality protocols and for statistical purposes only,[3] to link UMETRICS data to administrative and survey data housed at the US Census Bureau, as well as to patents, publications, and dissertations. Figure 3.2 provides an outline of the data architecture; a full description of the main data sources is in the Appendix 3.1 at the end of this chapter.

---

[2] Since the data are large and complex, this book contains many simplified assumptions. Given that others may want to replicate and test the robustness of our work, all the data and code that were used to generate the analysis are available to approved researchers. The UMETRICS data are available at the restricted data enclave at the Institute for Research on Innovation and Science (IRIS, iris.isr.umich.edu); the linked UMETRICS-Census data are available to approved researchers at the Federal Statistical Research Data Centers (FSRDC, www.census.gov/fsrdc).

[3] The data are protected under Title 13 and Title 26 of the US code. The data are for statistical use only; anonymized unique identifiers are used for match keys; and all results are reviewed to ensure that no identifiable information is disclosed.

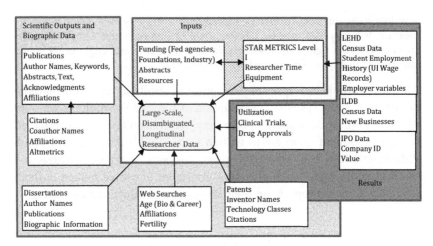

Figure 3.2. Data architecture

Briefly, data on grants and awards are derived from publicly available agency databases and are discussed in Chapters 4 and 5. Data on the workforce are derived from both UMETRICS data and matches to Census administrative and demographic data; these are discussed in Chapter 6. Earnings data are derived from the universe of W-2 and wage record data at the US Census Bureau. Placement data are derived from links to the Business Register (BR), which is the universe of US non-agricultural businesses and the source of data from which all other economic data are ultimately created; the Longitudinal Business Database (LBD), which is the universe of employer businesses; unique establishments in all industries and all US states linked over time; and the Integrated Longitudinal Business Database (iLBD), which is the universe of nonemployer businesses with links to employer universe (*16, 17*). The Census Bureau links enable us to identify the industry, characteristics, and geographic location of employers, to compare the employer characteristics with those of the US workforce at large. They are described in more detail in Chapter 7. Patent data are derived from links to the US Patent and Trademark Office (USPTO)'s recently developed, longitudinally linked, patent and inventor databases (patents-view.org) and are discussed in Chapter 8. Dissertation data are derived from ProQuest data, and are used throughout the empirical chapters. All of these data are combined to create the analytical dataset that provides the basis for the estimation of the regressions that are described in Chapters 9 and 10.

3.4.1 Development of a Comparison

One of the most exciting features of the new data infrastructure is the potential to create a comparison group – often called a counterfactual. In the model described in Section 3.2, the effect of a change in funding in food safety research (Z) on the subsequent economic and scientific activity of food safety researchers – particularly postdoctoral researchers and graduate students – should be compared with a reasonable comparison group.

The challenge becomes how to characterize that comparison group. The key idea is to compare the activities funded by awards that are quite similar to food safety research. Comparing all NIH grants to NIH food safety grants does not seem sensible; the NIH funds both basic and applied research that is very different in content and structure to food safety research. Similarly, the NSF not only funds food safety research, but also funds engineering, astrophysics, and computer science; comparing those grants does not seem sensible. Grants funded by US Department of Agriculture (USDA) are most likely to be similar to food safety research, but this approach to identifying a comparison is a relatively coarse one.

Our empirical approach is as follows. Identify (through the text analysis approach described in Chapter 4) both food safety grants and grants that are "not food safety." Also identify all grants associated with each funding program – NSF, NIH, and USDA. Then characterize "food safety funding programs" in two ways: (1) those that have funded at least one award that is for food safety (called "food safety funding program") and (2) those that have at least 5 percent of their funding portfolio in food safety (called "intense food safety funding program"). Then identify three possible comparison groups: One consists of grants funded by USDA that are "not food safety." The second includes grants that are "not food safety" in a food safety funding program. The third comprises grants that are "not food safety" in an "intense food safety funding program."

The last classification is worth describing in more detail. There are 120 programs where the abstract of at least one award is available. The counterfactual includes all researchers who were never funded by a food safety award, but were funded by a USDA nonfood safety award as well as those funded on an NIH or NSF award from a program where greater than 5 percent of the awards in UMETRICS were identified as food safety (see Appendix 3.1 at the end of this chapter). The eligible programs included Biological Sciences at NSF (8 percent food safety) and NIH awards from Microbiology and Infectious Diseases Research (7 percent food safety), Allergy and Infectious Diseases Research (8 percent), Human Genome

Research (10.4 percent), Environmental Health (11.7 percent), Occupational Safety and Health (15.1 percent), Food and Drug Administration Research (43.8 percent), and National Institute of Environmental Health Sciences (NIEHS) Superfund Hazardous Substances Basic Research (56.3 percent).

Thanks, then, to the combination of both UMETRICS and Census data, it is now possible to generate multiple comparison groups of individuals; each is used in subsequent chapters, first by developing an analytical sample consisting of graduate and students and postdoctoral researchers (discussed in more detail in Chapter 6). Specifically, the book examines only those who are at risk of being observed in our sample for the last 24 months prior to exit. This group is referred to as the "analytical sample" in subsequent chapters. Next examined are the workforce outcomes and the training environment of this group relative to the subset funded on food safety awards so as to contextualize the later more comparable subsets that are developed as alternate comparison groups.

3.5 Summary

Assessing the impacts of federal research funding in food safety research requires a multilayered interconnected data platform. This chapter details how those data are constructed and the necessary processes for linking data. A unique attribute of this data platform is the use of longitudinal business data from the Census Bureau, which allows the identification of industry and employee characteristics. In addition, the UMETRICS data are used to link from workforce activities back to the university research enterprise where federal dollars are dispensed with the purpose of creating new knowledge and innovative activities. Finally, this chapter carefully develops a comparison group of not-food-safety researchers, thereby supporting the assessment analysis that is shown in subsequent chapters in the book.

Appendix 3.1: Core Datasets

A3.1.1 UMETRICS Data

Currently, the UMETRICS data infrastructure is hosted at the Institute for Research on Innovation and Science (IRIS), which counts 50 research universities in its membership, with a forecasted membership of 150 by the end of FY 2017. The version of data used in this project contains data from 19 universities, of which 14 spanned a sufficient time period

(Northwestern, Ohio State University, Penn State, Purdue, Michigan State, New York University, and the Universities of Arizona, Hawaii, Illinois at Champaign-Urbana, Iowa, Kansas, Michigan, Missouri, Wisconsin) – representing approximately 30 percent of federal university-based R&D expenditures.

The UMETRICS data provide information on all the individuals supported on research funding by drawing the information from university human resource systems (*18*). It is based on the US STAR METRICS initiative, but has enhanced the available variables by including name and, in some cases, year and month of birth (*19*). It represents a new type of data collection in that it has evolved over a multiyear period; in particular, link assets have been added in response to a National Academies report, which noted: "Ongoing data collection efforts, including Science and Technology for America's Reinvestment: Measuring the Effect of Research on Innovation, Competitiveness and Science (STAR METRICS), could potentially be of great value if these datasets could be linked with other data sources and made more accessible to researchers" (*20*) (p. 51).

Although four files are provided by the universities, the key file of interest in this project is the employee file. For each federally funded project, the file contains all payroll charges for all pay periods (period start date to period end date) with links to both the federal award ID (unique award number) and the internal university ID number (recipient account number). Also available from the payroll records are the employee's internal de-identified employee number, the occupational classification, their full-time equivalent (FTE) status, and the proportion of earnings allocated to the award. These data enable researchers to capture all collaborations longitudinally as well as the network connections generated by the project. The file layout is shown in Table A3.1.

Both federal and nonfederal funding are covered in the data. The Catalog of Federal Domestic Assistance (CFDA), which is included in each award identifier, provides a full listing of all of the federal programs available to universities (and other types of organizations) and is captured in the UMETRICS data, so one can filter federal award expenditures by federal funding agency. The participating institutions also generated pseudo-CFDA codes to capture nonfederal sources of funding;[4] the bulk of these come from either private foundations or funding from the university's home state.

---

[4] Details on the nonfederal funding sources are provided here: www.starmetrics.nih.gov/static-2-1-0/Content/Downloads/Other-Funding-Source-(OFS)-Codes.xls.

Table A3.1   *UMETRICS Data Elements*

Data Element	Data Element Name	Definition
Period Start Date	PeriodStartDate	The start date for the period.
Period End Date	PeriodEndDate	The end date for the period.
Funding Source Name	FundingSource	Funding source assigned to each project – maps directly to funding code.
Unique Award Number	UniqueAwardNumber	Identifier specifying an award and its funding source, as defined by concatenating the 6-position funding source code – either the Catalog of Federal Domestic Assistance (CFDA) code or a STAR Other Funding Source (OFS) code – with an award identifier – either the federal award ID from the awarding federal agency (such as the federal grant number, federal contract number, or the federal loan number) or an internal award ID for nonfederal awards – with a space in between the two numbers
Recipient Account Number	RecipientAccount Number	Research Institution's internal number for the award.
Award Title	AwardTitle	Title of award.
Overhead Charged	OverheadCharged	Actual overhead dollars charged to the award in the specified period.
Total Direct Expenditures	TotalExpenditures	Total direct expenditures charged to the award in the specified period.
Campus ID	CampusId	Campus to which each award in assigned.
Sub-Organization Unit	SubOrgUnit	Subunit of university campus to which each award is assigned. The unit should be at the college level not at the level of the individual departments.

A3.1.1.1   Occupational Data

The UMETRICS data can be used not only to count the jobs at research organizations, but also to determine the occupational classifications and hence capture project-level workforce composition (*18, 21*). Because the data are drawn from payroll records, the universities provide the job

Table A3.2 *Examples of Graduate Student Job Titles from One University and Their Counts by Transaction and Unique Employee IDs*

Submitted Job Title	Classification	Total Transactions since 2007	Unique Employees (cells in this column can overlap)
Graduate Fellow	Graduate Student	2	2
Graduate Research Assistant	Graduate Student	18,306	2,068
Graduate Teaching Assistant	Graduate Student	3,327	673
Law Research Assistant	Graduate Student	28	7

Source: UMETRICS/STAR METRICS.

title, rather than the individual's occupation or educational category. Thus a major task for the project was to map the job titles into aggregated categories. The categories fall into two tiers. The first is classified as a subset of occupations (Faculty, Staff, Postdoctoral Researcher, Graduate Student, Undergraduate, and Other) based on the person's relationship to the university. In the second step, staff were classified into subcategories based on the nature of the work they conducted. These subcategories were Clinical Staff, Research Staff (staff members directly involved in conducting research, including Staff Scientists, Research Analysts, and Technicians), Research Facilitation Staff, Administrative/Coordinating Staff (including Research Support, Research Administration, and Research Coordinators), Instructional Staff (including instructional staff and academic specialists), Technical Support, and Other Staff (for people who could not be clearly classified into one of the descriptive categories).

Table A3.2 provides examples for one university of how job titles were matched to a particular classification of great interest – that of graduate student.

It is worth noting that the data are dynamic in nature, so individuals on research grants, particularly graduate students, do not fall neatly into an occupational category. An individual classified as a graduate student may or may not be a candidate for a PhD – and, given the nature of educational pathways, it may not be a fully meaningful distinction.

The challenges associated with creating occupational categories have, of course, a long history in labor economics (*22*). Most data on occupations come from worker self-reports, which are recorded and then coded into set categories by survey personnel. There are at least two sources of slippage in this process: (1) employees may describe what they do inaccurately and (2) survey personnel may record and/or code the responses with error. Indeed, occupation classifications on surveys are notoriously noisy. Mellow and Sider (1983) find that only 83.3 percent of Current Population Survey (CPS) respondents' major (one-digit) occupations match their employer's reports, and that share falls to 59.7 percent for detailed (three-digit) occupations (and these rates are considerably lower than for industry of employment, at 85.4 percent and 93.1 percent for detailed and major industry) (*23*). Our approach is markedly different insofar as it infers occupations from job titles obtained from university human resources.

A3.1.2 Census Data

The UMETRICS data linked to Census microdata on individuals, establishments, and firms have been made available to approved research projects through the Federal Statistical Research Data Center (FSRDC) network in FY 2017.

A3.1.2.1 Individual Data

Placement and earnings are derived from a match of UMETRICS data to the data from the US Census Bureau. The employee data are assigned a unique, protected identifier used internally by the Census to match individuals across multiple data sources for statistical and research purposes. The protected identifier is assigned probabilistically using name, date of birth, and location. In all cases, the data are anonymized by removing the employee's personal information from the file after the protected identifier is assigned (*24*). Approximately 95 percent of IRIS employees paid by federal or nonfederal grants are assigned a unique protected identifier (called a Protected Identification Key, or PIK).[5] Once the identifier is assigned, the UMETRICS employee data can be linked to a number of Census microdata assets, including the 2010 Decennial Census, the Individual Characteristics File, and the job-level Longitudinal Employer-Household Dynamics (LEHD) data

---

[5]   When the algorithm returned multiple PIK matches for an individual, that individual was not included in the analysis. When one PIK was assigned to multiple employee IDs, one employee ID was randomly selected.

(*25, 26*). These data provide information on demographic attributes including place of birth, household characteristics, employment outcomes, and earnings outcomes.

A3.1.2.2 Longitudinal Employer-Household Dynamics (LEHD) Data

The data that enable us to match workers with past and present employers, as well as their earnings, has been assembled at the LEHD program at the US Census Bureau (*26*). This database consists of quarterly records of the employment and earnings of almost all individuals from the unemployment insurance systems of all US states – these records provide the key link between workers and firms. This type of data has been extensively described elsewhere (*27*), but it is worth noting LEHD data have several advantages. In particular, the earnings are quite accurately reported, since there are financial penalties for misreporting. The data are current, and the dataset is extremely large. One limitation of the data is that there are no direct data links between workers and *establishments*, only between workers and *firms*. Thus, one cannot tell with certainty in which particular establishment a worker is employed if the employing firm consists of more than one establishment, which is true of about 30 percent of the workforce. Thus, probabilistic links are used to impute a place of work for workers who work for multiunit businesses.[6]

A3.1.2.3 Census Business Register

This dataset provides information about the characteristics of the businesses where individuals get jobs. It consists of the universe of US nonagricultural businesses and is the frame underlying all other Census business data.[7] The LBD and the iLBD are longitudinally linked, edited, and enhanced employer and nonemployer versions of the BR,

---

[6] These probabilistic links have been estimated in the LEHD data using multiple imputation techniques, based on a model that takes into account the relative location of workers and establishments, the employment distribution across establishments, and the dynamic employment restrictions imposed by worker and job flow dynamics.

[7] The key source data elements in the Business Register are (1) the SS-4, by which a new business tells the IRS whether it is beginning as a sole proprietorship, partnership, corporation, or personal service corporation; the state or foreign country in which it is incorporated; and whether it is applying because it is a new entity, has hired employees, has purchased a going business, or has changed type of organization (specifying the type) and (2) the 1120S K-1 series, which provides information on corporate shareholders (*30*).

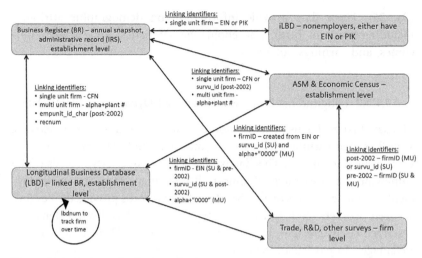

Figure A3.1. Links to the Business Register

respectively (*28*). They provide a longitudinal database that allows one to track firm performance, births, and deaths over time. These data are quite granular. For instance, it is possible to identify the specific establishments at which people work and classify establishments into 1,065 six-digit North American Industrial Classification System (NAICS) industries. See Figure A3.1.

A3.1.3   Construction of Links between UMETRICS and Census Data

Figure A3.2 shows a schematic of these data and the links between them.

A3.1.4   The Analytical File

The construction of the file is as follows for both UMETRICS individuals and the "comparison" file of non-UMETRICS individuals.

The employer identification number (EIN) codes for the universities were identified, compiled from the university website and Internal Revenue Service (IRS) records for nonprofit organizations. Then a combined LEHD-W2 worker history file was created that consists of PIK-EIN-Year and W-2 earnings and LEHD earnings. The PIK-EIN links are collected directly from the W-2 forms, while the PIK-EIN links in the LEHD file are created by linking the Employee History File (EHF), which lists the employee (PIK) and

Linking R&D and Innovation

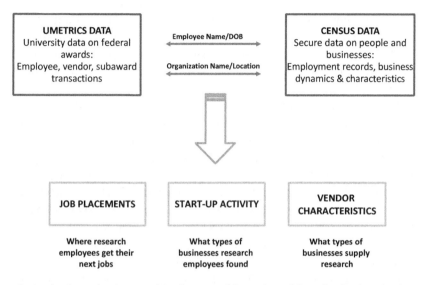

Figure A3.2 UMETRICS – Census Data Links Framework

state EIN code. Because the state EIN code can reference multiple establishments within a multi-unit firm (and in some cases, multiple firm IDs), the
establishment of the worker is first identified by linking the EHF file with the
Unit-to-Worker impute file (U2W). This approach identifies the establishment of the worker based on the first imputation, which is an SEINUNIT
number. The state EIN and SEINUNIT numbers are then linked to the
Employer Characteristics File (ECF) to obtain the exact EIN for the employee.

Some undergraduate employees (those on work-study) are not included
in the LEHD file. In this case, their record was linked to the W-2 file;
information gaps were then filled in with the LEHD data. The resulting
combined file goes from 2005 to 2014; each observation is a PIK-EIN-
Year-Earnings record.

University workers are identified by merging in the 37 EIN codes to the
combined LEHD-W2 file.. Once all of the workers are identified, including
UMETRICS individuals, the full work history for each PIK (protected
identification key) was derived by merging the PIKs back into the combined LEHD-W-2 worker history file. This provides the observation list.

At this stage, there are 31 million observations of PIK-EIN-Year-
Earnings. The data are then populated with individual characteristics

and firm-level characteristics. Demographic characteristics are derived from the Individual Characteristics File. Firm-level characteristics are a bit more complicated. The geographic codes (state FIPS, county FIPS, Census tract) are derived from the ECF file and attached to the UMETRICS file. This allows us to match the employer with firm-level data housed in the Longitudinal Business Database (LBD) and Business Register (BR).

The linkage to the LBD and BR is performed through the EIN-Geocode-Year identifiers. The EIN and 11-digit Geocode are collected from the BR, while the LBD contains a 5-digit Geocode. A direct match is made to the augmented UMETRICS file by EIN-Geocode combination (5-digit or 11-digit Geocode, depending on what is available and what can be linked), yielding a set of establishment and firm characteristics. The characteristics include industry, employment and payroll information (LBDNUM-Year-EIN-Geocode-Employment-Payroll-NAICS) for each firm. It is worth noting that the Geocodes are not always populated and the LBD contains nonfarm private businesses. It may also be the case that the universities are not included on the BR; in this case university characteristics cannot be included.

The LBD-BR file can then be combined with the university leavers file by EIN-Geocode-Year. The result is a file that contains the full earnings history and firm/industry variables for all individuals affiliated with UMETRICS UM universities. The last step involves identifying university EINs in the dataset that were not matched to the LBD/BR, which is achieved through a full list of university EINs provided by multiple sources, including the Integrated Postsecondary Education Data System (IPEDS) and the Carnegie Institute, supplemented with IRS data on tax-exempt institutions.

A3.1.5 Dissertations

The ProQuest Dissertations & Theses (PQDT) database includes more than 3 million citations and PDFs of full text for 1.6 million graduate works. More than 1,000 graduate schools are represented in the database, spanning 1861 to the present. The database includes abstracts from July 1980 forward for dissertations, abstracts from 1988 forward for master's theses, with PDF availability for every title from 1997 forward.

The complete ProQuest data include many types of degrees for which dissertations are submitted. They include literature, education, chemistry, engineering, psychology, business, economics, history, philosophy, sociology, and information science. The records contain information on the name(s) of the author(s) of the dissertation, title, number of pages, abstract and subject of the dissertation, university or institutions awarding the graduate degree, the graduate degree awarded, and the advisor's name, among others. While individuals may appear multiple times in the data, this number is small, and for the purpose of statistical matching, dissertation records are treated as if they corresponded to unique individuals.

The linkage process was conceptually straightforward. All institution IDs associated with universities within the scope in the ProQuest table were identified; individuals associated with those universities and identified as graduate students were then used for the match. The match was based on the first initial of individual's last name, corporate name, individual's first and last name, and degree year for all authors graduated from universities, using the Fellegi Sunter approach (*29*).

References

[1]   J. Lane, J. Owen-Smith, R. Rosen, B. Weinberg, New Linked Data on Research Investments: Scientific Workforce, Productivity, and Public Value. *Res. Pol.* **44** (9), 1659–1671 (2015).

[2]   P. Stephan, in *Innovation Policy and the Economy*, volume 7, J. Lerner, S. Stern, eds. (MIT Press, 2007).

[3]   K. B. Whittington, J. Owen-Smith, W. W. Powell, Networks, Propinquity, and Innovation in Knowledge-Intensive Industries. *Adm. Sci. Q.* **54**, 90–122 (2009).

[4]   D. Warsh, Economic Principals (2012), available at www.economicprincipals.com/issues/2012.12.23/1449.html.

[5]   National Research Council, *Data on Federal Research and Development Investments: A Pathway to Modernization* (National Academies Press, 2010).

[6]   P. E. Stephan, *How Economics Shapes Science* (Harvard University Press, Cambridge, MA, 2012).

[7]   R. B. Freeman, D. Goroff, *Science and Engineering Careers in the United States: An Analysis of Markets and Employment* (University of Chicago Press, 2009), www.nber.org/books/free09-1.

[8]   R. B. Freeman, Data! Data! My Kingdom for Data! Data Needs for Analyzing the S&E Job Market. *Support RAND* **32** (2004).

[9]   A. B. Jaffe, M. Trajtenberg, R. Henderson, Geographic Localization of Knowledge Spillovers as Evidenced by Patent Citations. *Q. J. Econ.* **108**, 577–598 (1993).

[10] S. Kantor, A. Whalley, Knowledge Spillovers from Research Universities: Evidence from Endowment Value Shocks. *Rev. Econ. Stat.* **96**, 171–188 (2014).

[11] P. Shu, The Long-Term Impact of Business Cycles on Innovation: Evidence from the Massachusetts Institute of Technology (2011).

[12] H. Sauermann, M. Roach, Science PhD Career Preferences: Levels, Changes, and Advisor Encouragement. *PLoS One* **7**, e36307 (2012).

[13]   A. J. Sumell, P. E. Stephan, J. D. Adams, in *Science and Engineering Careers in the United States: An Analysis of Markets and Employment*, R. Freeman, D. Goroff, eds. (2009).

[14]   E. J. Reedy, B. Litan, M. Teitelbaum, in *The Handbook of Science of Science Policy*, K. H. Fealing, J. Lane, J. H. Marburger, S. Shipp, eds. (Stanford University Press, 2011).

[15]   B. A. Weinberg et al., Science Funding and Short-Term Economic Activity. *Science* **344**, 41–43 (2014).

[16]   R. S. Jarmin, J. Miranda, "The Longitudinal Business Database," *Working Papers* (Center for Economic Studies, US Census Bureau, 2002), available at http://ideas .repec.org/p/cen/wpaper/02–17.html.

[17]   S. J. Davis et al., *Measuring the Dynamics of Young and Small Businesses: Integrating the Employer and Nonemployer Universes* (National Bureau of Economic Research, 2007).

[18]   J. I. Lane, J. Owen-Smith, R. F. Rosen, B. A. Weinberg, New Linked Data on Research Investments: Scientific Workforce, Productivity, and Public Value. *Res. Policy* (2015), doi:10.1016/j.respol.2014.12.013.

[19]   J. Lane, S. Bertuzzi, Measuring the Results of Science Investments. *Science* **331**, 678–680 (2011).

[20]   National Academy of Sciences, *Furthering America's Research Enterprise* (The National Academies Press, Washington, DC, 2014), www.nap.edu/openbook .php?record_id=18804.

[21]   N. Zolas et al., Wrapping It Up in a Person: Examining Employment and Earnings Outcomes for PhD Recipients. *Science* **360**, 1367–1371 (2015).

[22]   C. Conrad, W. Cheng, B. A. Weinberg, "University Occupation Classification: Technical Paper" (Columbus, Ohio, 2014).

[23]   W. Mellow, H. Sider, Accuracy of Response in Labor Market Surveys: Evidence and Implications. *J. Labor Econ.* 331–344 (1983).

[24]   D. Wagner, M. Layne, "The Person Identification Validation System (PVS): Applying the Center for Administrative Records Research and Applications' (CARRA) Record Linkage Software" (2014), available at www.census.gov/srd/ carra/CARRA_PVS_Record_Linkage.pdf.

[25]   J. M. Abowd et al., in *Producer Dynamics: New Evidence from Micro Data* (University of Chicago Press, 2009), pp. 149–230.

[26]   J. M. Abowd, J. Haltiwanger, J. Lane, Integrated Longitudinal Employer-Employee Data for the United States. *Am. Econ. Rev.* **94**, 224–229 (2004).

[27]   J. C. Haltiwanger, J. I. Lane, J. R. Spletzer, Productivity Differences across Employers: The Roles of Employer Size, Age, and Human Capital. *Am. Econ. Rev.* **89**, 94–98 (1999).

[28]   R. Jarmin, J. Miranda, "The Longitudinal Business Database," *CES Working Paper* (02–17, 2002).

[29]   I. P. Fellegi, A. B. Sunter, A Theory for Record Linkage. *J. Am. Stat. Assoc.* **64**, 1183–1210 (1969).

[30]   N. Greenia, K. Husbands Fealing, J. Lane, "Studying Innovation in Businesses: New Research Possibilities" (2008), available at www.irs.gov/pub/irs-soi/ 08rpinnovbusgreenia.pdf.

4

Identifying Food Safety–Related Research

Evgeny Klochikhin and Julia I. Lane

4.1 Overview

The discussion in Chapters 1 and 2, as well as the results of the expert workshop, made it clear not only that food safety is an interdisciplinary research area, but also that it is difficult even for experts to agree on what food safety is. The challenge is not unique to food safety, of course. Defining fields is a common challenge in science, dating at least as far back as Aristotle (1). And developing a taxonomy to describe fields of research is particularly challenging. To quote a working document prepared by SRI International for the National Center for Science and Engineering Statistics in 2012:

The current official standard for describing R&D activity in science, engineering and technology is The Office of Management and Budget (OMB) Directive No. 16, Standard Classification of Fields of Science and Engineering (FOSE), which first appeared in May 1978 in the Statistical Policy Handbook. The Directive has not been updated. The classification is organized around fields of science characterized as disciplines. The landscape of R&D activities has greatly changed since 1978. The scope of R&D activities has expanded beyond the traditional disciplines of science and engineering. New fields of R&D have emerged. R&D projects are often organized around broad national challenges, such as renewable (clean) and sustainable energies, cyber security, human health and safety, or technology areas such as robotics, bioinformatics, and nanotechnology. The outdated current classification does not adequately support this new landscape, nor does it capture the full breadth of R&D activities being conducted by the Federal Government. It does not include newer science disciplines, it does not enable description of inter/multi-disciplinary R&D activities, it does not support the flexible description of science from the perspectives of scientific discipline, socio-economic impact and enabling technologies, and it provides no clear mechanism for identifying emerging fields of R&D. (2)

In sum, current scientific taxonomies do not provide clear labeling for many new or interdisciplinary fields, including food safety–related research. This chapter describes how text analysis can be used to address the challenge in general, using food safety research as the case study. The chapter begins with a brief review of text analysis, then describes two technical approaches: search strings and wikilabeling. A discussion follows on applications to the grant and dissertation databases. Of particular interest is the human-driven validation, which is also discussed in detail. As always, the code and data are available for replication and reanalysis at the Institute for Research on Innovation and Science (iris.isr.umich.edu).

4.2 A Brief Review of Classification Approaches

The quality of data gathering for statistical purposes is largely compromised by the absence of clarity in the existing classification of fields of science (3). Survey respondents, data administrators, and persons responsible for tagging and curating knowledge products are required to use the taxonomy in their reporting activities even if the field categories do not describe their work.

The challenge, then, is how to develop a useful classification system. The role of a taxonomy is threefold (4). It serves a descriptive function in that it standardizes language, which enables coordination and knowledge building around the entities or concepts described by that language. It serves a classification function, in that it reveals connections and relationships among different areas of knowledge in predictable, useful, and commonly understood ways. And it serves a sense-making function, in that it overlays useful, common structure (or "semantics") onto the different fields of science, enabling analysts and policymakers to make sense of significant patterns and relationships within that domain, including the identification of gaps in knowledge, and the basis for structuring testable hypotheses.

Computer scientists have been reasonably successful in moving beyond manual classification systems (5, 6). Here we review two approaches that have been successfully used in this context.

Approach 1: Wikilabeling. Wikilabeling represents a group of information retrieval and clustering techniques that are used to identify topics within a given corpus based on the words used in the documents in the corpus and their copresence as articles within the well-known online encyclopedia, *Wikipedia*. This improves on topics that come solely from the corpus (endogenous topics), in that the titles of articles are curated by humans as they review an enormous underlying corpus and thus represent legitimate, institutionalized topics. This method is highly automated so that little human intervention is required to come to a set of results.

The main way this is done is through using a subset of an externally developed encyclopedia, *Wikipedia*, as a source of topics. Because *Wikipedia* is constantly being updated, it represents a human-curated set of topics that are always up to date, and leveraging this existing investment drastically increases the value of the final output without additional human intervention on the part of the authors. Many of the developments in this area have come from work on the Semantic Web and Linked Data. For example, Meij et al. mapped search queries to the DBpedia ontology (derived from *Wikipedia* topics and their relationships) and found that this could enrich the search queries with additional context and concept relationships (7).

The strength of wikilabeling is that it not only is capable of deriving the list of potential labels from within the corpus but can also help to induce existing taxonomies such as the categories used in the National Science Foundation (NSF) Survey of Research and Development Expenditures at Universities and Colleges. Double-labeling of scientific documents provides an opportunity for cross-walk between existing classification and the new taxonomy derived directly from the corpus. Thus, the approach may point at potential routes as to how conventional categories can be improved to reflect the latest scientific developments.

The crucial component of the method consists in the ability to evaluate the similarities between individual documents and *Wikipedia* articles to see what concepts and methods are mentioned and applied in the respective research projects (see Figure 4.1).

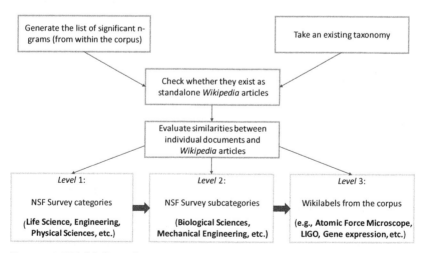

Figure 4.1 Wikilabeling schematic

This technique is of interest for two reasons. First, the ontology based on *Wikipedia* reflects a set of classification decisions made on very large scale and over an extended period of time. Second, the derivation of the ontology from an actively curated encyclopedia and the density and nature of the links mapped between concepts carry some assurance of salience to the community at large. In contrast to other methods, such as topic modeling, this technique for machine-assisted classification carries a significant exogenous reference point for the classification decisions.

The method has the further advantage that it is capable of inducing topics derived both from within the corpus and from external sources. This process allows us to construct natural hierarchies based on the language used in the scientific documents and in respective *Wikipedia* articles. The labels are used to describe both established and emerging fields of science and engineering as they are referenced online.

Wikilabeling is a predominantly unsupervised technique; that is, it requires no training data and needs limited human intervention. It relies significantly on the available corpora and does not need any additional textual data. In this, the approach offers significant flexibility and can provide guidance for updating existing taxonomies and identifying new and emerging fields of science and engineering. Thus, the method seeks to address all four challenges of data gathering and analysis in that it allows for largely unsupervised classification of scientific documents, their descriptive analysis, and sense-making.

Approach 2: Topic Modeling (supervised hierarchical latent Dirichlet allocation). Topic modeling has allowed for quick, inexpensive understanding of large datasets (8) and has been extensively applied to scientific documents. Blei and Lafferty (9) used dynamic topic models to show how physics progressed from discussions of the ether, to relativity, to quantum mechanics, to string theory. Dietz et al. (10) showed that topic models recapitulate the information gleaned from citations. Hall et al. used topic models to mark trends such as the growth of statistics in natural language processing (11). Ramage et al. used topic models to determine which universities lead and lag in creating new ideas (12). Unsupervised topic models generate distributions of related words observed over a collection of documents that are thematically related.

The core idea is a "generative" story: It posits a process of how the documents came to be. In this context, each document is assumed to be a mixture of a small number of topics, and each word is associated with one of the topics. The story has missing pieces, so-called latent variables that must be discovered using probabilistic inference. These latent variables

Table 4.1 *Topic Examples*

Geology	Mantle, crust, plate, depth, earth
Genetics	Genes, gene, genetic, genome, chromosome
Cancer	Cancer, tumor, p53, damage, tumors

include the namesake topics of topic models: the words that appear together to form coherent themes. When we apply posterior inference to discover the topics that best explain an observed dataset such as articles in the journal *Science*, we can discover coherent topics, such as those exemplified in Table 4.1.

Topic models have been used to characterize scientific disciplines at the National Institutes of Health (NIH) (*13*), in student theses (*14*), and at the National Academy of Sciences (*15*). However, in our experience, topic modeling is not useful to identify predefined areas (like food safety), so we use the approach primarily for validation rather than classification.

Evaluation: All categorizations, generated either by wikilabeling or topic modeling, must subsequently be validated, and we draw on the existing literature to do so. There are two types of accepted validation approaches that we can notionally call query-side validations and retrieval-side evaluations.

Scientometric studies widely use query-side validation: For example, Porter et al. (*16*) organized a number of workshops and expert interviews to make sure that their search string used to retrieve nanotechnology-related publications was robust. The major advantage of this approach is that it provides upfront rigor and reduces the probability of retrieving multiple irrelevant documents.

The computer science literature typically uses the retrieval-side evaluation. Several methods are typically benchmarked against a random baseline and similar methods to define how many relevant documents have been retrieved in each case (*17*). If the new method shows better results, it is then considered a valid contribution. Purity, or precision and recall, is one of the most widely used criteria in this evaluation. It is defined as the extent to which the machine classification results are consistent with a prior human proxy for tagging content. In statistical terms, this measure is aligned with the familiar Type I (false positive) and Type II (false negative) errors. Precision is formally defined as

$$\text{Precision} = \frac{|\,\{\text{relevant documents}\} \cap \{\text{retrieved documents}\}\,|}{|\,\{\text{retrieved documents}\}\,|}$$

Recall is computed as

$$\text{Recall} = \frac{|\ \{\text{relevant documents}\} \cap \{\text{retrieved documents}\}\ |}{|\ \{\text{relevant documents}\}\ |}$$

Both approaches have known limitations. The query-side validation is prone to error due to differing search interfaces presented by existing databases as well as clustering error. For example, Web of Science and Scopus can return rather different results based on a similar search string. The reasons typically lie in the underlying database structure and the application programming interface (see more in Chapter 9). Clustering error means that a minor inaccuracy in the search string is likely to return many irrelevant documents, which would be recognized as systematic outliers in the retrieval-side evaluation.

In its turn, the retrieval-side evaluation is highly reliant on user expertise and availability of the "ground truth" data. Scholars often lack both when working with scientific documents: User evaluation requires significant level of respondent familiarity with the subject, which is hard to achieve in rather specialized fields (in other words, it is hard to expect an ordinary person to reliably distinguish between an agricultural science research paper about pesticides and a food safety one). Ground truth (prelabeled) data are also a luxury in scientific literature analysis. Many curated corpora used by computer scientists are news items (e.g., the Reuters Corpus and TREC data sets), congressional records, and colloquial language (e.g., the Naval Postgraduate School chat corpus) (*18*).

4.3 Approach

The study relied on traditional search string approach and wikilabeling to identify food safety research, drawing on the data described in Chapter 3. Topic modeling was used to validate the selection.

4.3.1 Search Strings

The *search term strategy* uses regular expressions and Boolean logic to search for relevant documents. This approach draws on earlier work that used search term strategies to identify interdisciplinary research (*19, 20*). This method is useful to discover a wide range of documents that use a given vocabulary and therefore can have potential relevance to the subject in focus.

The initial challenge was to identify a list of relevant food safety terms from existing encyclopedic ontologies. The chosen ontology was *Wikipedia*, which has an advantage in that it provides structured knowledge via page redirects, links to other *Wikipedia* pages and other web resources, and user-defined categories assigned to individual pages. An additional advantage is that *Wikipedia*'s accuracy is on par with the other more established knowledge repositories, such as *Encyclopaedia Britannica* (21).

The specific search string steps to identify food safety awards are as follows:

1. Choose an "anchor" article for a given research field: The "Food safety" page is a logical entry point to the *Wikipedia* tree of food safety–related research.
2. Identify all intrawiki links to other *Wikipedia* pages in the "anchor" article: for example, "Food processing," "Food poisoning," "Listeria," etc.
3. Identify all intrawiki links to second-level *Wikipedia* pages linked to the ones identified in the previous step: for example, "Food processing" links to "Fish processing," "Slaughterhouse," "Canning," etc.
4. Explore any other specialized resources for additional terms: for example, www.foodsafety.gov and the Food Safety Research Information Office at the US Department of Agriculture (USDA) National Agricultural Library.
5. Compile a complete list of discovered terms from the titles of *Wikipedia* pages and combine it with any additional ones from other sources.
6. Ask experts to review the resultant list and select only relevant terms.
7. Manually categorize the terms into bigger buckets for ease of use and comprehension.

The original list of concepts retrieved from *Wikipedia* comprised more than 700 terms, many of which are generic and ambiguous, such as "nutrition," "health," and "pathogen." Although related to food safety research, these terms can also be used in other broader fields, such as health sciences and medicine, and hence can be considered redundant. The search strings were also reviewed by expert workshop participants and irrelevant ones were pointed out; for example, "Acesulfame potassium" is a sugar substitute and is more relevant to nutrition rather than food safety.

The final list includes almost 300 concepts retrieved from *Wikipedia* and other sources and divided into six main categories: (1) General (two terms): "food safety," "food security";[1] (2) food pathogens (119 terms): "*Coxiella burnetii*," "*Yersinia pseudotuberculosis*," "*Aspergillus parasiticus*," etc.; (3) biochemistry and toxicology (41 terms): "acid-hydrolyzed vegetable protein," "hydrogenated starch hydrolysate," "forensic toxicology," etc.; (4) food processing and preservation (51 terms): "active packaging," "irradiation," "frozen food," etc.; (5) food safety management and food policy (56 terms): "contaminated food," "Federal Meat Inspection Act," "hazard analysis and critical control points," etc.; and (6) food-related diseases (20 terms): "foodborne illness," "diarrhea," "listeriosis," etc.

4.3.2 Wikilabeling

As noted in Section 4.2, the approach represents a group of information retrieval and clustering techniques that are used to identify topics within a given corpus based on the words used in the corpus documents and their copresence as articles within the well-known online encyclopedia, *Wikipedia*.

The particular approach used to identify food safety research using text categorization was to compare documents to semantic model vectors of *Wikipedia* pages constructed using WordNet (22). These vectors account for the term frequency and their relative importance, given their place in the WordNet hierarchy, so that every token within the vector is assigned a specific value, defined here as

$$SMV_{wiki}\,(s) = \sum_{w \in Synonyms(s)} \frac{tf_{wiki}(w)}{\mid Synsets(w) \mid}$$

where w is a token within *wiki*, s is a synset that is associated with every token w in WordNet hierarchy, *Synonyms(s)* the set of words (i.e., synonyms) in synset s, $tf_{wiki}(w)$ is the term frequency of the word w in the *Wikipedia* article *wiki*, and *Synsets(w)* is the set of synsets for the word w.

The overall probability of a candidate document d (e.g., an NSF award abstract or a publication abstract) matching the target query, or in our case a *Wikipedia* article *wiki*, is

---

[1] It should be noted that food security research can be rather distinct from food safety. To further restrict our search strategy to only relevant documents, the researchers added several additional constraints, as described in the next subsection. For example, the full regular expression for the general terms is as follows: *((food safe*) OR (food secur*)) NOT (hung* OR nutrit* OR calor*)*.

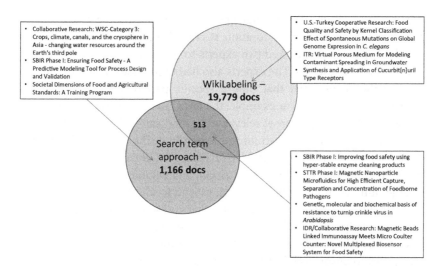

- Collaborative Research: WSC-Category 3: Crops, climate, canals, and the cryosphere in Asia - changing water resources around the Earth's third pole
- SBIR Phase I: Ensuring Food Safety - A Predictive Modeling Tool for Process Design and Validation
- Societal Dimensions of Food and Agricultural Standards: A Training Program

WikiLabeling – **19,779 docs**

- U.S.-Turkey Cooperative Research: Food Quality and Safety by Kernel Classification
- Effect of Spontaneous Mutations on Global Genome Expression in *C. elegans*
- ITR: Virtual Porous Medium for Modeling Contaminant Spreading in Groundwater
- Synthesis and Application of Cucurbit[n]uril Type Receptors

513

Search term approach – **1,166 docs**

- SBIR Phase I: Improving food safety using hyper-stable enzyme cleaning products
- STTR Phase I: Magnetic Nanoparticle Microfluidics for High Efficient Capture, Separation and Concentration of Foodborne Pathogens
- Genetic, molecular and biochemical basis of resistance to turnip crinkle virus in *Arabidopsis*
- IDR/Collaborative Research: Magnetic Beads Linked Immunoassay Meets Micro Coulter Counter: Novel Multiplexed Biosensor System for Food Safety

Figure 4.2. Combination of search and wikilabeling: example

$$wiki_{BEST} = \sum_{w \in doc} max_{s \in Synsets(w_t)} SMV_{wiki}(s)$$

where $Synsets(w_t)$ is the set of synsets for the word w_t in the target document *doc* (e.g., NSF award abstract) and $SMV_{wiki}(s)$ is the semantic model vector of a *Wikipedia* page, as already defined here.

Figure 4.2 shows an example of how the wikilabeling and search term approaches are combined to identify food safety grants in the NSF portfolio.

4.4 Validation

This study applied both types of validation approaches described here to ensure that the most relevant documents related to food safety research would be identified.

4.4.1 Query-Side Validity

As noted, the researchers originally retrieved more than 700 potentially relevant food safety search terms from *Wikipedia* using the approach described in Section 4.3.1. This list contained terms that were either very specific (e.g., "*Listeria*" and "*E. coli*") or too broad (e.g., "Egg" and

"Raw meat"). While plainer language terms generally can be removed by a nonexpert reviewer, expert curation is critical for the more specific keywords. The researchers asked two experts to review the list and define only the most relevant terms. The experts also had to provide constraint phrases in case they considered that only a specific part of selected concept is relevant to food safety: For example, the term "food security" can be rather broad and have only narrow relevance to food safety. The expert recommended that the study constrain the search by using the following string: *((food safety) OR (food securit*)) NOT ((hung*) OR (nutrit*) OR (calor*))*. Excluding the topics of hunger, nutrition, and calories, the study removed a large number of false positives irrelevant to food safety.

After this thorough review the researchers presented the list to an expert group participating in the workshop organized under this project (see Chapter 2). The group helped further refine the term list and underlying categories to ensure validity of the final search string. Among others, the experts pointed out that the topic of food quality can be largely irrelevant to food safety unless it directly related to sanitary norms and food pathogen detection.

It is also important that genetically modified food is not a topic directly related to food safety. The final search string includes additional constraints to ensure the relevance of identified documents: *(((ill*) OR (disease) OR (hazard*)) AND ((genetically modified food*) OR (GM food) OR (genetic engin*)))*.

As a result of this expert review, the final list includes almost 300 concepts retrieved from *Wikipedia* and other sources that were used to construct the final query to retrieve food safety–related award abstracts.

4.4.2 Retrieval-Side Evaluation

Retrieval-side evaluation provides the most precise error rate in terms of precision and recall. However, it has limited utility for correction of these errors unless used iteratively. In other words, retrieval-side evaluation demonstrates the overall performance of the developed method but cannot be easily converted to recognize the patterns driving the systematic errors.

Document-level evaluation is the most widely used technique in computational linguistics (23). Computer scientists typically use crowdsourced platforms, such as Mechanical Turk and Crowdflower, for relevance assessment and evaluation (24). Users are asked to review individual documents from a given corpus. Next, they can assign their own labels (categories) to those documents, select a label from a predefined list, or evaluate whether the machine-assigned label is correct. Depending on the experiment design user responses are used as the "ground truth" data set to either train an algorithm or evaluate how well it performed in assigning correct labels to the documents. While acceptable for general evaluation, common users are not always able to recognize the nuances of scientific documents. Expert involvement is needed to assess the relevance and robustness of the approach.

A designated experimental environment needs to be set up to evaluate the validity of retrieved food safety documents. The researchers set up a special website at www.foodsafetyresearch.net to conduct the evaluation. The study proceeded from the assumption that its method might have retrieved some documents that were in fact not food safety–related ("false positives") or could have missed a number of relevant documents ("false negatives"). Given that the researchers have the population of award abstracts from 2000 to 2014 for three U.S. agencies (NIH, NSF, and USDA), it is possible to create a random sample from both retrieved and unretrieved documents.

The testing sample consisted of 100 documents: 50 award abstracts that were identified as food safety–related and 50 award abstracts from the set of unretrieved documents (i.e., presumably not food safety–related).[2] However, the size of the retrieved and unretrieved samples is quite different, which can create bias. For example, 513 out of 180,316 NSF awards in 2000–2015 were identified as food safety–related. To make the test more robust, the researchers randomly selected 50 abstracts from the retrieved set and 50 abstracts from the set of documents identified by either wikilabeling or search term strategy but not both.

The research team contacted a number of food safety research experts – identified both through the workshop and through personal contacts. Ten agreed to participate in the retrieval-side evaluation by reviewing up to 20 abstracts each and answer a simple question: Is the abstract food safety-related or not? If they found food safety–related documents among the unretrieved sample, this was classified as Type II error. In contrast, if the reviewer found some of the retrieved documents as not food safety–related, this was classified as Type I error. The results were mixed. While many of the tags seemed correct, a number did not. For example, the following awards were tagged as nonfood safety–related: "Mastitis resistance to enhance dairy food safety," "Food safety and animal health,"

---

[2] Note that to lower the burden for reviewers, the sample was reduced proportionately to 20 documents in total.

"Fluorescence-based chemical sensor for saxitoxin,"[3] and "Controlling staphylococcus aureus virulence by way of the pentose phosphate shunt."[4] Such classification inconsistencies are not unusual in the field; a typical approach to improve reliability of human evaluation is to present the same evaluation sample to several reviewers (25). However, given the challenges of recruiting multiple expert respondents with food safety backgrounds, the researchers decided to consider other methods to conduct a retrieval-side evaluation.

The particular approach chosen to strengthen the validation is a *cluster-level* validity check. In essence, the researchers used topic modeling to identify the overarching topics among retrieved food safety documents. The underlying assumption is as follows: If the generated topics are irrelevant, then there is high probability that large clusters of retrieved documents have not been selected correctly and have therefore been characterized as false positives. In other words, given that one topic has a high probability of describing a given set of documents within the corpus, then an irrelevant topic will be a likely indicator of a systematic error (say, 30 topics per 500 documents would mean that each topic is likely to describe 500/30, or about 17 documents; i.e., every irrelevant topic likely means that about 17 of retrieved documents are potentially irrelevant).[5]

The topic modeling approach based on latent Dirichlet allocation (26) was used to categorize the identified food safety awards. Table 4.2 presents the top five topics by the number of food safety grants funded by each agency. In all, 30 topics were generated for the NSF and 100 topics each for the NIH and USDA awards.[6] The topics generally confirm the results of the clerical review performed in the previous state: The NSF mostly funds biological science and technology-focused food safety research; the NIH focuses on bacteriology, biochemistry, and the medical aspects of food safety; and the USDA funds research directly related to food science, food microbiology, and farm-to-fork projects. In the meantime, the topics also

---

[3] Saxitoxin is a paralytic shellfish toxin consumed with food.

[4] *Staphylococcus aureus* is a major cause of foodborne disease in the United States.

[5] These numbers are used here for illustrative purposes only. The topic modeling algorithm has a different rationale of discovering the latent variables behind textual data. Returned topic probabilities are, however, often distributed equally across all topics, as reported in the Mallet software output.

[6] Latent Dirichlet allocation does not provide clear guidance how the number of topics should be defined. The rule of thumb is that a smaller number of documents will likely be better represented by a smaller number of topics, given the clustering nature of the algorithm. Therefore, 30 topics would be more representative of the 513 NSF awards, while 100 topics are a good choice for about 4,000 NIH and USDA awards.

Table 4.2 *Top Five Topics of Food Safety Awards by Federal Agency*

Top Five Topics	Number of Food Safety Awards per Topic
NSF	
detection pathogen detect bacteria assay contamination toxin diagnostics sensor biosensor real-time technology array coli pathogenic foodborne monitoring impact salmonella	46
plant student science understanding use data health result important human specie cell provide effect system crop including program also	32
genome gene genomics undergraduate http database sequencing dna www organism generated sequence genomic researcher edu trait outreach website analysis	32
pathogen gene mutant undergraduate pathway protein signaling arabidopsis effector bacterial biochemical immunity disease interaction investigator cellular postdoctoral strategy kinase	30
fungi fungal evolutionary fungus dna alternaria virus asexual diversity strategy wasp filamentous genus cryptomycota researcher grisea symbiosis organism interaction	26
NIH	
accreditation fda iso laboratory iec microbiological regulatory funding manufactured microbiology analytical outbreak proficiency surveillance analysis mfrps wsda lab capability	157
nutrition trainee veterinary epidemiology investigator biomedical nutritional toxicology disease cnru discipline master infectious graduate physiology biochemistry funded interdisciplinary career	127
foodborne regulatory outbreak strategy ehs-net inspection fda implementation mfrps conformance surveillance manufactured implement illness establishment restaurant contamination funding database	105
ehec coli toxin intestinal pathogen o157 bacterial stx epec virulence stec epithelial strain gene diarrhea inflammatory characterize stx2 effector	104
allergy asthma allergic atopic allergen ige infant outcome disease sensitization dermatitis airway cohort pediatric immunology exposure maternal asthmatic symptom	88

(*continued*)

Table 4.2 (*continued*)

Top Five Topics	Number of Food Safety Awards per Topic
USDA	
pathogen contamination foodborne processor microbial haccp strategy ass intervention consumer hazard evaluate salmonella risk stakeholder validation poultry producer coli	120
pathogen salmonella foodborne poultry food-borne outbreak contamination environment antimicrobial illness post-harvest bacteria pre-harvest consumer pre pathogenic treatment coli elimination	107
foodborne consumer behavior foodservice educator ass evaluate implement illness grocery outreach handler risk participant strategy targeted module disseminate restaurant	105
waterborne pathogen disease niaid water-borne foodborne food protozoa virus organism threat protecting bacteria microbiology bioterrorist consortium implemented inter-disciplinary botulism	97
fresh-cut processed microbial pathogen technology vegetable fruit treatment microorganism sensory irradiation evaluate inactivation spoilage antimicrobial pathogenic strategy non-thermal packaging	90

indicate that the resultant documents may include award abstracts from adjacent scientific fields, such as nutrition and agricultural sciences. While these documents do not necessarily fall under the strict definition of food safety, they can be considered part of a broader food science agenda with potential implications for food safety (e.g., specific ways of raising cattle and crop might have specific relation to human-consumed food in the farm-to-fork cycle).

4.5 Summary

This chapter presents the application of a computational approach to identifying food safety research. The approach facilitates the identification of interdisciplinary and emerging science and technology research, such as food safety. Three stages were involved. The first was to combine two machine learning and information retrieval techniques to identify candidate grants. The second was validation through expert curation. The third was to apply additional computational techniques – latent Dirichlet allocation – to validate the results.

Overall, food safety–related research is present in about 0.3 percent of the NSF, 0.4 percent of the NIH, and 6 percent of the USDA awards (see Chapter 5). Topic modeling shows that some of the identified awards are related to scientific fields adjacent to food safety research. Some of these disciplines, such as bacteriology and nutrition, may contribute to food safety, especially within the farm-to-fork cycle, and hence are considered generally relevant for this study. It is important to note that the work described in this chapter represents an illustrative rather than a definitive approach. The results can and should be replicated and expanded by the research community; experts routinely disagree on the boundaries of fields, and food safety research is no exception.

References

[1]   M. Manktelow, History of Taxonomy. *Lect. from Dept. Syst. Biol. Uppsala Univ.* (2010), http://atbi.eu/summerschool/files/summerschool/Manktelow_Syllabus.pdf.

[2]   SRI International, "Working Experts Session on Characterizing and Measuring Fields of Research in Science and Engineering" (2012).

[3]   OECD, "Revised Field of Science and Technology (FOS) Classification in the Frascati Manual" (Paris, France, 2007), available at www.oecd.org/science/inno/38235147.pdf. Accessed August 27, 2017.

[4]   H. Roitblatt, A. Kershaw, P. Oot, Document Categorization in Legal Electronic Discovery: Computer Classification vs. Manual Review. *J. Am. Soc. Inf. Sci. Technol.* **61**, 70–80 (2010).

[5]   National Science Foundation, "Report to the Advisory Committees of the Directorates of Computer and Information Science and Engineering and Social, Behavioral and Economic Sciences" (National Science Foundation, 2011).

[6]   E. Klochikhin, P. Lambe, A Better Way to Classify Science. *Res. Fortnight* (2015).

[7]   J. Meij, M. Bron, B. Huurnink, M. Hollink, L. de Rijke, *ISWC '09: Proceedings of the 8th International Semantic Web Conference* (2009).

[8]   S. Gerrish, D. M. Blei, "A Language-Based Approach to Measuring Scholarly Impact," in *Proceedings of the 27th International Conference on Machine Learning (ICML-10)* (2010).

[9]   D. Blei, J. Lafferty, in *Text Mining: Classification, Clustering, and Applications,* A. Srivastava, M. Sahami, eds. (Chapman & Hall, 2009).

[10] L. Dietz, S. Bickel, T. Scheffer, "Unsupervised Prediction of Citation Influences," in *Proceedings of the 24th International Conference on Machine Learning.* (ACM, 2007).

[11] D. Hall, D. Jurafsky, C. D. Manning, "Studying the History of Ideas Using Topic Models," in *Proceedings of the Conference on Empirical Methods in Natural Language Processing – EMNLP '08* (2008), p. 363.

[12] D. Ramage, C. D. Manning, D. A. Mcfarland, *Proceedings of NIPS Workshop on Computational Social Science and the Wisdom of the Crowds* (2010).

[13] E. Talley et al., Database of NIH Grants Using Machine-Learned Categories and Graphical Clustering. *Nat. Methods.* **8** (2011).

[14] T. L. Griffiths, M. Steyvers, in *Latent Semantic Analysis: A Road to Meaning*, T. Landauer, D. McNamara, S. Dennis, W. Kintsch, eds. (Lawrence Erlbaum, 2006).

[15] D. M. Blei, J. D. McAuliffe, A Correlated Topic Model of Science. *Ann. App. Stat.* 17–35 (2007).

[16] A. L. Porter, J. Youtie, P. Shapira, D. J. Schoeneck, Refining Search Terms for Nanotechnology. *J. Nanoparticle Res.* **10**, 715–728 (2008).

[17] R. Ghani, M. Schierholz, in *Big Data and Social Science: A Practical Guide to Methods and Tools*, I. Foster, R. Ghani, R. Jarmin, F. Kreuter, J. Lane, eds. (Taylor & Francis, 2016).

[18] S. Bird, E. Klein, E. Loper, *Natural Language Processing with Python: Analyzing Text with the Natural Language Toolkit* (O'Reilly Media, 2009).

[19] R. N. Kostoff, J. S. Murday, C. G. Y. Lau, W. M. Tolles, The Seminal Literature of Nanotechnology Research. *J. Nanoparticle Res.* **8**, 193–213 (2006).

[20] P. Shapira, J. Wang, Follow the Money. *Nature* **468**, 627–628 (2010).

[21] J. Giles, Internet Encyclopaedias Go Head to Head. *Nature* **438**, 900–901 (2005).

[22] R. Navigli, S. Faralli, A. Soroa, O. De Lacalle, E. Agirre, *Proceedings of the 20th ACM International Conference on Information and Knowledge Management* (ACM, 2011), pp. 2317–2320.

[23] J. Boyd-Graber, E. A. Klochikhin, in *Big Data and Social Science: A Practical Guide to Methods and Tools*, I. Foster, R. Ghani, R. S. Jarmin, F. Kreuter, J. I. Lane, eds. (Taylor & Francis, 2016).

[24] O. Alonso, S. Mizzaro, *Proceedings of the SIGIR 2009 Workshop on the Future of IR Evaluation* (2009), vol. 15, p. 16.

[25] L. J. Cronbach, Coefficient Alpha and the Internal Structure of Tests. *Psychometrika* **16**, 297–334 (1951).

[26] D. Blei, A. Ng, M. Jordan, Latent Dirichlet Allocation. *J. Mach. Learn. Res.* 993–1022 (2003).

5

The Structure of Research Funding

Reza Sattari, Julia I. Lane, and Chia-Hsuan Yang

5.1 Overview

Describing food safety research at any given point in time faces at least three empirical challenges. The first is due to the heterogeneity of the field; as noted in Chapter 2, funding for food safety research is allocated across diverse disciplines, multiple institutions, and different funding sources. The second is due to the reporting structure; food safety research is not one of the standard categories reported by universities to the National Center for Science and Engineering Statistics via the Higher Education Research and Development (HERD) survey.[1] The third is due to accounting differences, because reported funding in any field captures obligations reflecting a snapshot in time, rather than ongoing expenditure over time. Thus, it does not describe the portfolio of active research in any field.

This chapter provides a description of the way in which different features of the UMETRICS data can be used to address each of these challenges. The heterogeneity of the field is addressed through combining data across universities and funding agencies. Although our study is necessarily a partial analysis of each, the approach is fully scalable as the UMETRICS program expands scales. The text analysis approach described in Chapter 4 can be used to categorize research in nonstandard categories. And because the UMETRICS data are transaction based, they capture all activities (at least, as measured by active spending) during the period of the grant.

The combination of these features enables the exploration of the complexity and dynamics of funding for food safety research in a new way.

---

[1] The HERD survey, under the authority of the National Science Foundation Act of 1950, collects the R&D expenditures at US college and universities by research fields (www .nsf.gov/statistics/srvyherd/).

A combination of university and agency data can be used to show that researchers are typically funded from multiple sources, over multiple years, that grants and contracts support multiple individuals. This enables one to describe the connections across funding sources and puts food safety research in context. An important advantage is that the structure of the data also leads to identification of grants that are closely related to food safety research in terms of the types of researchers who are supported; this is then used to characterize a comparison group of researchers.

This chapter also describes a variety of empirical challenges. Text analysis is possible only if text is provided, and although some agencies are now providing public descriptions of the work that taxpayers have funded, many still do not. This chapter documents and discusses the implications of these lacunae. Even though a "grant" or "award" is a conceptually straightforward concept, it can be challenging to measure empirically. Not only do different agencies have idiosyncratic funding structures but also transaction data like UMETRICS can be difficult to link across sources.

5.2 Data

The university data include information about funds from all sources, including federal agencies such as the Department of Defense, Department of Energy, Environmental Protection Agency, NASA, and the Department of Education. However, because the focus here is on academic research, the study excluded grants to small businesses (e.g., Small Business Innovation Research [SBIR]), training grants, and the National Science Foundation's (NSF's) Major Research Infrastructure grants.[2] The study included research-oriented grants (referred to as research awards in this chapter).

To study food safety research, the study combined UMETRICS data with public award data from three different agencies to portray the funding structure in food safety fields: the NSF, the National Institutes of Health (NIH), and the US Department of Agriculture (USDA). These agencies are the primary supporters of food safety research, and they provide publicly available abstract information.[3] Each agency is described in more detail later in this chapter.

---

[2] These are the awards that have "training," "small business," "infrastructure," "loan," or "federal work-study program" phrases in their titles.

[3] The data are a part of the Open Government Initiative issued by President Obama on December 8, 2009. Federal agencies are required to take specific actions to promote transparency, participation, and collaboration, which includes publishing government information online and improving the quality of government information.

The funding structures can be documented because, as noted in Chapters 3 and 4, UMETRICS data includes a grant identifier. It is therefore possible to link that identifier to detailed information about the grant in the public award data provided by the funding agencies. The resulting grant information includes the text description, the start and end dates, and the dollar amount of the grant. Thus, it is possible to describe the number and types of grants available for food safety research.

Several facts are worth noting about funding data from agencies:

1. Agency reporting is not typically standardized. NSF grants can be both standard (all obligated in a given year) and continuing (the obligated amount spread over multiple years). The reporting of NIH grants is extraordinarily complex, reflecting the idiosyncratic administrative systems of 27 different institutes. The total amount of obligated funds is typically reported for each year the grant is active.
2. Grants are dynamic in nature, so the period of performance can be extended due to no-cost extensions or supplemental funding.
3. Some grants are very complex. In the case of NIH, for example, a popular funding mechanism is a program project grant (what NIH calls a P01), in which an umbrella program (with one project number) can have multiple projects (each with separate numbers). Azoulay et al. provide an excellent overview of the complexity of NIH funding (*1*). In the case of the USDA, one type of grant is Hatch Act funding. It supports continued, multidisciplinary agriculture research crossing different institutions and in multiple states. This grant does not have direct ties to individual projects.
4. Some funding mechanisms are complicated. In the case of the NSF, for example, multiple institutions can submit the same grant collaboratively to avoid incurring multiple overhead charges. Each institution will have a different grant number assigned for the same grant.

For the purposes of this chapter, the UMETRICS identifier is the "unit" of analysis, recognizing that future work should and will develop richer characterizations of grant awards.

National Science Foundation. The NSF is an independent federal agency that supports fundamental research across all fields of science and engineering (S&E) and S&E education. The agency is the funding source for approximately 24 percent of all federally supported fundamental research conducted by American colleges and universities. Each year, NSF receives about 50,000 requests for funding proposals for research, education, and training projects, making about 11,500 of new funding awards each year to the most competitive applicants. Information about research projects funded by NSF since 1989 can be found by searching NSF's Award Abstracts database (www.nsf.gov/awardsearch/).

National Institutes of Health.[4] The NIH is an agency of the US Department of Health and Human Services and is the primary federal agency responsible for biomedical and health-related research. "NIH's mission is to seek fundamental knowledge about the nature and behavior of living systems and the application of that knowledge to enhance health, lengthen life, and reduce illness and disability." To accomplish this mission, the NIH both conducts its own scientific research through its Intramural Research Program and provides major biomedical research funding to non-NIH research facilities. The NIH is composed of 27 separate institutes and centers, each responsible for different disciplines of biomedical science.

US Department of Agriculture. Projects are conducted or sponsored by USDA research agencies, state agricultural experiment stations, land grant universities, other cooperating state institutions, and participants in grant programs. The USDA funds research through the Agricultural Research Service, the National Institute of Food and Agriculture (NIFA), the Economic Research Service, and the Forest Service. Some research is supported through "formula funds" (e.g., Hatch, Evans-Allen, and McIntire-Stennis), which are sometimes reported in aggregated form for the entire land grant university or other institution.[5]

5.2.1 Linkage Approach

Linking administrative data to public grant data from agencies can sometimes be problematic. Universities keep track of award identifiers, but their data systems do not necessarily contain all of the elements of the unique identifier that enable precise linking. Even the agencies themselves may use different identifiers or format of identifiers to indicate grants or awards from different programs. Funding mechanisms are also inherently complicated, and hence some common elements are used for linkage – for example, award title, award recipients (principal investigator and coprincipal investigator) – may not link data effectively. For example, one award

---

[4] Much of this description was taken from the agencies' websites, which are in the public domain.
[5] For more information on project types and research programs supported by National Institute of Food and Agriculture (NIFA), see https://nifa.usda.gov/programs.

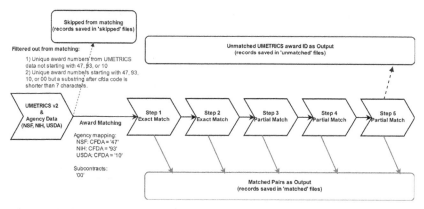

Figure 5.1 UMETRICS empirical linking approach
Source: N. Nichols, C.-H. Yang, "A QA Report on Award Matching Process" (Ann Arbor, Michigan: Institute for Research on Innovation and Science, 2016) (2).

title can indicate multiple grants, and one grant crossing multiple years can also be associated with multiple award titles as the project evolves or gets extensions.

The empirical linking approach is as follows. The internal UMETRICS award identifier was used to link to the public federal award number by the relatively intuitive matching process illustrated in Figure 5.1. Step 1 identified awards that have an identifier that is identical to the agency ID. The identifiers are then normalized (all special characters and spaces are removed and all nonnumeric characters were converted to lowercase characters). Exact matches were identified in Step 2 using the normalized identifiers. Step 3 identified partial matches using the longest substring in order to capture cases where the agency ID was longer than the university identifier. Step 4 identified partial matches using the agency ID as the longest substring, which captured any matches where the university identifier had a longer character length than the agency ID. Step 5 identified partial matches using chopped internal identifier as longest substring. Finally, all matches were hand validated.

5.3 Basic Facts

The UMETRICS data are transaction data, so individuals appear multiple times on multiple awards. Over the period of study, there were almost 8,750,000 transactions. About 270,000 individuals were supported on more than 117,000 awards to the 19 universities in the study. About 46,000 of

Table 5.1 *Counts of Grants by (Federal Agency) and Type (Food Safety Classification)*

	All Nonfood Safety Grants	Food Safety		
		Only Search	Only Wiki	Union of Search and Wiki
NIH	16,165	162	473	606
NSF	14,955	97	179	269
USDA	1,402	274	182	371
Total	32,522	533	834	1,246

these grants are made by NSF, NIH, and USDA; of these, about 33,000 have abstracts that are suitable for text analysis and that can be matched to the agency source. The match rates are very different by agency – about 90 percent of NSF awards and can be matched, but only two-thirds of NIH awards and can be matched. About 60 percent of USDA awards that are not Hatch Act block-funded and can be matched. About half of the USDA grants in our scope[6] are Hatch Act block funding, which have no direct ties to individual projects and cannot be linked to the transaction data. Appendix 5.1 contains a detailed breakout of the different match rates by agency and decision rule.

Table 5.1 shows a summary of the awards classified by grant source, that is, agency and type (food safety or not). In the broadest view of food safety grants defined in Chapter 4 (the union of search and wiki methods), about 3 to 4 percent of awards can be classified as food safety; that is the food safety definition that this chapter will use going forward.

Table 5.1 also makes it clear that it is possible to use UMETRICS data to characterize both the food safety portfolio of agencies and the dominant sources of food safety funding. Thus, although more food safety awards are funded by NIH than by the other two agencies, these awards represent only about 3.8 percent of the NIH grants. By contrast, food safety grants make up a much larger proportion of the USDA portfolio: About 30 percent of the USDA grants that could be topic modeled and matched are food safety awards.[7]

[6] The grants received by the 19 institutions in the public USDA award datasets during the same data coverage time span in UMETRICS data (for each institution).
[7] In this study, 46 percent of USDA grants are Hatch Act block funding, which have no direct ties to individual projects and cannot be linked to the transaction data. Thus, those grants cannot be identified through the linkage approach.

One of the most exciting features of the new data infrastructure is the potential to create a comparison group. In the model described in Chapter 3, the effect of a change in funding in food safety research (Z) on the subsequent economic and scientific activity of food safety researchers – particularly postdoctoral researchers and graduate students – should be compared with a reasonable comparison group.

The challenge becomes how to characterize that comparison group. The key idea is to compare the activities funded by awards that are quite similar to food safety research. Comparing all NIH grants to NIH food safety grants does not seem feasible; the NIH funds both basic and applied research that is very different in content and structure to food safety research. Similarly, the NSF, which also funds food safety research, funds engineering, astrophysics, and computer science; comparing those grants does not seem feasible either. USDA-funded grants are the most likely to be similar to food safety research, but the comparison is a relatively coarse one. A major advantage of UMETRICS data is that these data can be used to identify the funding of researchers who are doing work similar in nature to that being done by food safety researchers. The core notion is that while it is unlikely that a research program in economics would be making decisions about whether or not to fund food safety research, it is highly likely that specific research programs in the NIH or NSF – and almost all USDA programs – could potentially fund food safety research. One can use UMETRICS data to identify these research programs, then use the nonfood safety awards that are being funded by those programs as food safety comparison groups.

The study's empirical approach is as follows. The text analysis approach described in Chapter 4 was used to identify both food safety grants and grants that were "not food safety." They also identified all grants associated with each funding program – the NSF, NIH, and USDA. Then "food safety funding programs" can be characterized in two ways – those that have funded at least one award that was classified as food safety (called "food safety funding program") and those that had at least 5 percent of their funding portfolio in food safety (called "intense food safety funding program"). The researchers then identified three possible comparison groups. One comprises grants that were funded by the USDA that were "not food safety." The second consists of grants that were "not food safety" in a food safety funding program. The third comprises grants that are "not food safety" in an "intense food safety funding program."

The last classification is worth describing in more detail. There are 120 programs where the abstract of at least one award is available. The comparison group includes all researchers who were never funded by a food safety award but were funded by a USDA nonfood safety award as well as those funded on a NIH or NSF award from a program where greater than 5 percent of the awards in UMETRICS were identified as food safety (see Appendix 5.2). The eligible programs included Biological Sciences at NSF (8 percent food safety) and NIH awards from Microbiology and Infectious Diseases Research (7 percent food safety), Allergy and Infectious Diseases Research (10 percent), Human Genome Research (11 percent), Environmental Health (12 percent), Occupational Safety and Health (15 percent), Food and Drug Administration Research (44 percent), and National Institute of Environmental Health Sciences (NIEHS) Superfund Hazardous Substances Basic Research (56 percent). Appendix 5.2 provides a list of all the comparison programs, as well as an illustrative list of a few of the programs below the 5 percent threshold.

Subsequent chapters will explore how the combination of both UMETRICS award data and employee data, as well as US Census data, enables the generation of multiple comparison groups of individuals.

5.4 Funding over Time

Another advantage of the UMETRICS data is that it is possible to examine the active food safety portfolio in each year. This is important because even if funding is obligated in one year, the expenditures extend for several years beyond the grant. As a result, an increase in funding that occurs in one fiscal year can take three or more years for the full effort to take effect; the reverse is true for decreases.

Table 5.2 shows the differences in terms of obligated project lengths between projects initially funded by different agencies and by type in 2012. Awards funded by the NSF and the USDA, compared with the NIH, are twice as likely to last one year or less. Looked at another way, one-third of NIH-funded awards last five years or more, compared with less than a quarter of awards funded by the USDA or NSF.

Agencies also differ in terms of the size of the grants, as shown in Table 5.3. While more than half of the awards funded by the NSF are less than $250,000, the majority of awards funded by the NIH or USDA are between $250,000 and $1,000,000. This is particularly true for the USDA, as Table 5.3 shows. The table also shows that more than half of the food safety awards, as well as the comparison awards, are between $250,000 and $1,000,000.

UMETRICS data permit some insights into the dynamics of funding as well. For example, in 2012, there were 469 active food safety awards in our

Table 5.2 *Obligated Length of Grants Initially Active in 2012*

Project Length	Agency				Type	
	NIH	NSF	USDA	NIH, USF, and USDA	Food Safety	Comparison
1 year or less	93	104	18	215	10	31
2 years	314	156	13	483	18	53
3 years	237	145	20	402	16	63
4 years	250	193	39	482	20	76
5 years or more	432	179	31	642	36	73
Total	1,326	777	121	2,224	100	296

Note: Counts of grants initially active in 2012, matched to agency files and not missing project length.

Table 5.3 *Obligated Amount of Grants Initially Active in 2012*

Obligated Amount in $	Agency				Type	
	NIH	NSF	USDA	NIH, USF, and USDA	Food Safety	Comparison
0–100K	137	170	19	326	12	31
100K–250K	353	217	21	591	20	67
250K–1 mil	697	357	69	1,123	58	169
> 1 mil	139	33	12	184	10	29
Total	1,326	777	121	2,224	100	296

Note: Counts of grants initially active in 2012, matched to agency files and not missing obligated amount

data. There are 143 food safety grants that were initiated in that year, and 118 that ended (Table 5.4). Clearly, there is an ongoing "churn" of the food safety grant portfolio and accompanying "churn" as people begin or complete food safety projects.

Chapter 7, which focuses on the structure and dynamics of the individuals on the teams working on food safety research, will examine this churn in more detail.

5.5 The Context of Food Safety Research

Many principal investigators receive funding from multiple agencies to support their research, and the resulting connections can be quite rich. Chapter 7 will describe the structure of research teams in much more detail; this section simply describes the degree to which food safety

Table 5.4 *UMETRICS Awards in 2012*

	Awards from All Agencies	Matched Awards from NIH, NSF, and USDA	Food Safety	Comparison
Currently active	31,303	10,346	469	1,433
First year	12,524	3,099	143	457
Last year	9,019	2,613	118	335

Note: Counts of all grants active in 2012, including those missing obligated amount and project length

Table 5.5 *Connections between Food Safety Grants and Other Funding Sources*

	All	Nonfood Safety	Food Safety	Comparison
Research awards in UMETRICS	117,150	32,522	1,246	4,105
Connected to at least one other award	71,636	24,553	876	2,845

research is connected to other research within the institution. The relationship between two grants can be characterized in many ways; for the purposes of this chapter, two grants are connected if they have at least two people in common. Of course, the richness of the data allows for many different definitions – additional filters could include, for example, the length of time that individuals overlap or the peer relationships (e.g., both graduate students or faculty). A full exploration of such work is left to other researchers.

A total of about 71,000 out of the more than 117,000 UMETRICS research-focused awards are connected to at least one other award (Table 5.5). Similarly, about 70 percent of the topic-modeled awards are connected to another award; there are very similar degrees of connectedness for both food safety awards and the comparison group.

In general, conditional on being connected to at least one other award, a typical award is connected on average to more than 16 other awards. Interestingly, this number is higher for food safety awards compared with their comparison group. Food safety awards on average are connected to 21.45 other awards, whereas their comparison group peers are connected to 14.15 other awards. Tables 5.6 and 5.7 provide a summary of number of awards that are connected to different types of awards by their topic and their agencies, respectively. Food safety awards, when compared with their comparison group, are more likely to be connected to the awards that are

Table 5.6 *Connections of Food Safety Awards to Other Fields*

		All Awards	Food Safety Awards	Comparison Awards
Average Number of Awards Connected to		16.72	21.45	14.15
By Topic	**Nonfood Safety**	5.54	8.17	3.55
	Nonfood Safety – Comparison	0.56	2.25	3.05
	Food Safety	0.26	2.04	0.69
	Not Topic Modeled	10.35	8.99	6.86

Table 5.7 *Connections of Food Safety Awards to Those Funded by Other Agencies*

		All Awards	Food Safety Awards	Comparison Awards
Average Number of Awards Connected to		16.72	21.45	14.15
By Agency	Funded by **NIH**	6.18 (36.9%)	12.04 (56.1%)	6.03 (42.6%)
	Funded by **NSF**	1.52 (9.1%)	1.19 (5.5%)	1.04 (7.3%)
	Funded by **USDA**	0.43 (2.5%)	1.12 (5.2%)	1.35 (9.5%)
	Funded by **other agencies**	8.58 (51.3%)	7.11 (33.1%)	5.73 (40.5%)

( ) = The percentage of award connections by agency within each type of award.

funded by NIH (56.1 vs. 42.6 percent) and less likely to be connected to the awards that are funded by NSF and USDA.

5.6 Summary

This chapter describes the technical approach used to match two data sources – UMETRICS data and publicly available data from funding agencies. The resulting data will allow researchers to set up a credible empirical strategy by constructing comparison groups that are reasonably comparable with food safety researchers.

The chapter also provides basic facts regarding the funding structure of food safety research, specifically about its length, obligated funds, and funding sources. It also provides insight on how the food safety research environment differs from other research environments in terms of connectedness to other research projects within an institution.

Appendix 5.1: Match Rates by Agency and Decision Rule

Table A5.1 *Match Rates by Agency and Decision Rule*

Data Source			NIH	NSF	USDA
Text Analysis	Projects		1,044,707	180,822	60,764
	Awards		872,851	180,822	16,963
Crosswalk	Projects		48,283	24,115	3,100
	Awards		40,846	21,599	3,005
Combined Text	Projects		42,915	21,837	3,097
Analysis and Crosswalk	Awards		36,805	19,792	3,002
Employee	Awards		20,363	16,054	1,785
Transaction File	Research	All	18,181	15,952	1,778
Merged with	Awards	Correct CFDA	17,796	13,312	1,606
Combined Text		Sub-Award	380	2,603	171
Analysis and Crosswalk		Incorrect CFDA	5	37	1
Employee Transaction	CFDA Research Awards		29,154	16,046	5,663
Match Rate 1 (Correct CFDA)			61.0%	83.0%	28.4%
Match Rate 2 (All)			61.5%	85.4%	30.5%
Employee Transaction	CFDA Research Awards less Non-Abstract Programs		29,154	16,046	5,023
Match Rate 3 (Correct CFDA)			61.0%	83.0%	32.0%
Match Rate 4 (All)			61.5%	85.4%	34.2%
Employee Transaction	CFDA Research Awards less Programs < 5 Topic-Modeled Awards		29,154	16,046	3,464
Match Rate 5 (Correct CFDA)			61.0%	83.0%	46.4%
Match Rate 6 (All)			61.5%	85.4%	48.9%
Employee Transaction	CFDA Research Awards less Programs < 10 Topic-Modeled Awards		29,154	16,046	3,297
Match Rate 7 (Correct CFDA)			61.0%	83.0%	48.7%
Match Rate 8 (All)			61.5%	85.4%	51.3%
Employee Transaction	CFDA Research Awards less Programs < 10 Topic-Modeled Awards		29,154	16,046	3,408
Match Rate 9 (Correct CFDA)			61.0%	83.0%	47.1%
Match Rate 10 (All)			61.5%	85.4%	49.7%

Appendix 5.2: Comparison of Funding Programs

Table A5.2 *Comparison of Funding Programs*

Program Title	Agency	Award Counts (less Excluded)			
		Total Award	Topic Model	Food Safety	Food Safety/Topic Model
Food Safety and Security Monitoring Project	NIH	8	8	8	100%
Refugee and Entrant Assistance_Wilson/Fish Program	NIH	7	1	1	100%
NIEHS Superfund Hazardous Substances_Basic Research and Education	NIH	50	16	9	56%
Food and Drug Administration_Research	NIH	93	32	14	44%
Integrated Programs	USDA	167	71	30	42%
Biomass Research and Development Initiative Competitive Grants Program (BR&###)	USDA	11	5	2	40%
International Science and Education Grants	USDA	14	12	4	33%
Agriculture and Food Research Initiative (AFRI)	USDA	561	242	69	29%
Homeland Security_Agricultural	USDA	27	15	4	27%
Beginning Farmer and Rancher Development Program	USDA	16	9	2	22%
Biotechnology Risk Assessment Research	USDA	14	9	2	22%
Higher Education – Institution Challenge Grants Program	USDA	54	27	6	22%
Secondary and Two-Year Postsecondary Agriculture Education Challenge Grants&###;	USDA	9	9	2	22%

(continued)

Table A5.2 (*continued*)

| Program Title | Agency | Award Counts (less Excluded) | | | Food Safety/Topic Model |
		Total Award	Topic Model	Food Safety	
Grants for Agricultural Research_Competitive Research Grants	USDA	389	285	53	19%
Cooperative Extension Service	USDA	357	116	20	17%
Specialty Crop Research Initiative	USDA	63	19	3	16%
Organic Agriculture Research and Extension Initiative	USDA	36	13	2	15%
Occupational Safety and Health Program	NIH	242	146	22	15%
Higher Education à Graduate Fellowships Grant Program	USDA	33	27	4	15%
Agricultural Research_Basic and Applied Research	USDA	938	8	1	13%
Grants for Agricultural Research, Special Research Grants	USDA	520	298	37	12%
Environmental Health	NIH	436	281	33	12%
Human Genome Research	NIH	211	130	14	11%
Allergy and Infectious Diseases Research	NIH	2,063	1,236	129	10%
Biological Sciences	NSF	1,777	1,296	98	8%
Microbiology and Infectious Diseases Research	NIH	208	83	6	7%
Blood Diseases and Resources Research	NIH	279	180	9	5%
National Center for Research Resources	NIH	263	141	7	5%
Trans-NIH Recovery Act Research Support	NIH	1,282	1,059	50	5%
Diabetes, Digestive, and Kidney Diseases Extramural Research	NIH	1,733	1,133	48	4%
Lung Diseases Research	NIH	715	501	21	4%
Cancer Cause and Prevention Research	NIH	1,021	604	25	4%
Trans-NIH Research Support	NIH	170	108	4	4%

Program Title	Agency	Award Counts (less Excluded)			Food Safety/Topic Model
		Total Award	Topic Model	Food Safety	
Research on Healthcare Costs, Quality, and Outcomes	NIH	343	223	7	3%
Nursing Research	NIH	322	228	7	3%
Cancer Centers Support Grants	NIH	191	99	3	3%
Geosciences	NSF	1,750	1,481	44	3%
Cancer Biology Research	NIH	560	414	12	3%

References

[1] P. Azoulay, J. S. G. Zivin, D. Li, B. N. Sampat, Public R&D Investments and Private-Sector Patenting: Evidence from NIH Funding Rules. *Natl. Bur. Econ. Res. Work. Pap. Ser.* **No. 20889** (2015), doi:10.3386/w20889.

[2] N. Nichols, C.-H. Yang, "A QA Report on Award Matching Process" (Ann Arbor, Michigan: Institute for Research on Innovation and Science, 2016).

The Food Safety Research Workforce and Economic Outcomes

Matthew B. Ross, Akina Ikudo, and Julia I. Lane

6.1 Overview

A key theme of this book is that people are at the core of the research enterprise. Funding agencies recognize this through their actions. Research funding acts to direct the research skills and research interests of both seasoned researchers and new PhDs toward that area (*1, 2*). Research also serves as a mechanism for training the next generation of investigators. In particular, funding in a field supports principal investigators, who then train graduate students in the process of doing their own research. Not only does research funding affect the current productivity of a field, but it also has a lasting impact that accumulates over time.

The relationship between the production of PhDs and the future of a research field is caused by the fact that the number of PhDs has a direct impact on the research produced in a field. Paula Stephan, in a series of papers and a recent book, has pointed out that relative salaries and demographics, as well as the availability of financial support, affect the production of PhDs (*3, 4*). The effect of demographic diversity on the creation and transmission of new ideas has been the focus of a great deal of discussion (*5, 6*), with the National Science Foundation (NSF) and the National Institutes of Health (NIH) emphasizing the importance of diversity in their mission statements (*7*). Recent research on doctoral recipients has linked UMETRICS with US Census data to document employment and earnings outcomes and the demography of graduate students employed on research awards (*8, 9*).

This chapter establishes some basic facts about the current workforce composition of food safety research, relative to several comparison populations, with a particular focus on graduate students and postdoctoral researchers. The chapter documents the number of individuals working on food safety research in the dataset, and describes the construction of the analytical sample to be used in the empirical analysis. Additional details describe the number of faculty, graduate students, and postdoctoral researchers working in the field and contrast these to other fields of research. The chapter then turns to examining the demographic composition of the workforce and compares those demographics with those in other fields as well as a comparison population.

6.2 What Is Currently Known

There is a vast literature on the importance of demographics and diversity to the production of science. That literature has focused on three main characteristics: age, gender, and foreign-born status.

The link between scientific productivity and age was succinctly summarized by Jones and Weinberg (*10*), who noted that two factors were important:

(1) How the training requirements related to acquiring foundational knowledge may explain the age at which scientific careers begin, and (2) the distinction between conceptual and experimental work in explaining creative peaks across the life cycle. Although we do not identify causal mechanisms, we show that measures drawn from this prior work, in addition to a measure of foundational knowledge based on backward citation ages, all move in a striking and intuitive way with shifts in the tendency for scientific contributions by the young. These collective dynamics are especially pronounced in physics during the early 20th century. (*10*)

Numerous studies have examined gender differences in productivity (*11–15*). The existing literature has not studied whether during graduate school, that is, at the earliest stage of a scientist's professional career, there are differences in publication output conditional on gender. Further, there has been little research on the effect of systematic gender variation in graduate students' professional environment on publication outcomes. What is known is that even small early-career differences in productivity can have substantial later-career effects, given what is known concerning processes of cumulative advantage and positive feedback mechanisms (*14, 15*).

The aging of the scientific workforce has attracted a great deal of attention for two reasons. One is that older researchers have been thought to be less productive, although that finding may be more related to training requirements and the nature of research than to chronological age (*10*). The second is simply the replacement of retiring scientists by new scientists – as the saying goes, "Science advances one funeral at a time" (*18*).

There is a substantial literature on the link between foreign-born status and economic activity (*19*). Immigration of highly skilled scientists and researchers has had important ramifications for US economic development – Jones (*20*) finds that long-run economic growth is significantly affected by workers specialized in research and development (R&D). Kerr and Kerr (*21*) note that immigration is a particularly important contributor to the highly skilled workforce. Indeed, since the mid-2000s, "immigrants have accounted for the majority of US workers in STEM [science, technology, engineering, and math] with doctoral degrees" (*22*).

Little is directly known about the link between research funding and the demographic characteristics of the doctorally qualified research workforce. Even in the Survey of Earned Doctorates, the main source of data on doctoral recipients, there is no question that fully characterizes support from federal research funding. Two questions provide indirect information: Question A5 asks, "Please indicate whether each of the following was a source of financial support during graduate school: fellowship/scholarship; grant; teaching assistantship; research assistantship; other assistantship; traineeship; internship; loans; personal savings; personal earnings; spouse's, partner's or family's earnings; employer reimbursement; foreign support." Question A6 asks, "Which two sources in question A5 provided the most support?" (*23*). UMETRICS fills a gap in the existing knowledge base regarding the training environment and research support that contributes to both the advancement of science and the training of the doctoral workforce.

However, preliminary work that has linked UMETRICS data to the Survey of Earned Doctorates to examine the link between federal funding and support for doctoral recipients had some intriguing findings (*23*). First, federal funding affects *who* does research in terms of gender and racial demographics. Of the women in the sample, 39% were federally funded, compared with 52% of men. There were also substantial differences across agencies – a larger share of doctoral recipients supported by NIH were women (50%), African American (2.6%), and Hispanic (4.2%), compared with the NSF, the Department of Defense, or the Department of Energy. Federal funding was also highly correlated with the pipeline of researchers going into certain fields, particularly R&D fields and the decision to pursue postdoctoral research.

6.3 Sample Construction

The core data of UMETRICS are unusually rich in that they can characterize the full workforce involved in producing research. The richness of the transaction data is due to the many dimensions along which it can be aggregated – including time, individual researcher, principal investigator, research teams, research field, and award.[1] But this richness has a drawback: A number of decisions need to be made in order to make the data analytically tractable and allow for inquiry into a specific set of research questions. This chapter details the decisions made in constructing our analytical sample and, in the process, describes the composition of the workforce.

One additional advantage of the UMETRICS data is that it better captures the entire constellation of teams engaged conducting research, including faculty, undergraduate and graduate students, postdocs, and staff. As noted in Chapter 3, data on the *full team of researchers* supported by individual research grants are captured in the transaction data provided by research institutions (*24*). This distinction is important, as most datasets describing scientific research typically only capture information on the principal investigators assigned to awards or projects (*2*). For our sample of 19 universities, with data ranging from the years 2001 to 2016, there are a total of 341,017 unique individuals who appear in the data. Based on an individual's dominant occupation, that is, the occupation where they spent the majority of their time, there were as many as 35,319 faculty, 79,317 undergraduate students, 68,631 graduate students, and 22,202 postdoctoral researchers. Across all years and occupations, there were a total of 125,776 individuals working on topic-modeled awards from NIH, NSF, and USDA. A total of 117,384 of these individuals were observed working on nonfood safety awards, while 8,392 individuals were working on food safety awards.

The nature of the dataset requires some careful thought about how to structure the analytical sample. Unlike surveys, the data are based on financial transactions, which are observed for all periods for which each university sends data. Some universities provided very long data ranges (the longest ranges from 2001 to 2016), but others were quite short

---

[1]   Recall that not all individuals working on research grants are included in the UMETRICS data. The employee transactional data only include people and employees paid on research grants. Individuals paid as work-study trainees and those on honoraria are not covered. Coverage on federal grants is generally complete, with the exception of one university that did not supply classified Defense Department research.

(e.g., 2013–2015). The transactional nature of the data thus presents an empirical challenge, because the data are necessarily both left-truncated (i.e., individuals cannot be observed prior to the date that the university provided data) and right-truncated (i.e., individuals cannot be observed subsequent to the last date that the university provided data). To describe the set of individuals who were engaged in research, particularly graduate students and postdocs, it was necessary to define a period within which that research occurred. Based on earlier research, a subset of the dataset was used to include only individuals whose institution transmitted data at least 24 months before the last year that they were reported as being paid in the UMETRICS data. Of the 341,017 individuals working on research grants, 90,833 were graduate students and postdocs. As shown in Table 6.1, the 24-month restriction, as well as examining only individuals who exited before 2014 so that workforce data from the Longitudinal Employer-Household Dynamics (LEHD) could be used, reduced the available set of individuals to 15,254. Of those 15,254 individuals, there were 8,327 who were observed working on grants from NIH, NSF, or USDA that had abstracts available for topic modeling.

As Table 6.1 illustrates, our analytical sample consists of 8,327 graduate students and postdocs, of whom 443 were observed on food safety awards and 7,884 were observed on nonfood safety awards. In the proceeding examination of demographic and basic workforce trends, food safety researchers were compared with the analytical sample overall, as well as with those funded on grants identified to be nonfood safety and those working on grants identified to be comparable (as discussed in Chapter 5). These individuals are the comparison group. Although individuals often work on multiple grants, individuals were included in the comparison

Table 6.1 *Sample Construction*

Individuals	All	Food Safety	Not Food Safety	
			All	Comparison
All	341,017	8,392	117,384	19,907
Faculty*	35,319	1,484	16,946	2,795
Graduate and Postdoc*	90,833	2,183	37,747	5,457
Analytical Sample	15,254	443	7,884	1,043
ProQuest Match	5,324	116	2,951	313
LEHD Match	9,400	250	5,000	600

* Unlike our construction of the analytical sample, individuals are tabulated based on their dominant occupation across all periods rather than the last 24 months in the data.

group only if they were not observed working on a food safety grant. In other words, the following analysis compares individuals who were ever funded on food safety grants with the individuals funded by food safety-intensive research programs but who were never observed on a food safety grant.

6.4 Demographic Characteristics

As described in Chapter 3, demographic data on the research workforce is derived from UMETRICS data matched with US Census administrative employment and demographic data. Here, the study describes the demographic and workforce composition of the analytical sample in terms of age, gender, race, place of birth, earnings, and employment.

6.4.1 Age, Gender, and Race

Understanding the demographic composition of any research workforce is important for a variety of reasons. An older workforce means that future funding might need to be targeted at junior researchers in order to have a pipeline of specialists in food safety. Less diversity, as measured by the underrepresentation of women, foreign-born individuals, and minorities, can result in less innovation. In the case of food safety research, our analysis suggests that there is very little difference in either the mean age or the age distribution between a workforce funded on food safety grants and one funded on nonfood safety grants, as shown in Table 6.2. When disaggregated into occupations, however, there are some differences between the food safety workforce and the comparison group. In particular, faculty and staff are somewhat older in the food safety research field, compared with those in the comparison group: The mean age of faculty is 53 in food safety and 50 in the comparison group. There is little to no difference in the mean age for students (postdoctoral researchers, graduate students, and undergraduate students) between the two groups.

There are, however, differences in the gender composition of the workforce. Figure 6.1 describes the gender composition of the food safety research workforce relative to the research workforce as a whole. About 60% of the overall workforce is male (this includes research assistants, administrative staff, and staff scientists, as well as faculty, postdoctoral researchers, and graduate students). Researchers in the food safety field are more likely to be female than the research workforce as a whole, with only

Table 6.2 *Mean Age by Occupation*

	Not Food Safety					
	NIH, NSF, USDA	NIH	NSF	USDA	Comparison	Food Safety
All	**32**	**33**	**31**	**32**	**33**	**33**
Faculty	50	51	49	51	50	53
Postdoc	36	36	36	36	36	36
Graduate	30	30	30	30	30	30
Undergraduate	24	24	24	24	24	23
Staff	36	36	35	40	36	38
Other	36	37	34	35	35	37

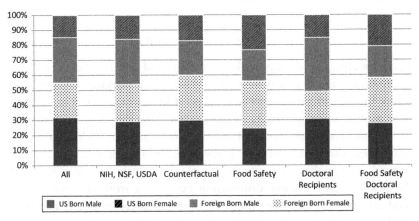

Figure 6.1 Workforce composition by gender and place of birth

about 45% being male. The proportion of female researchers in the comparison group falls between that for the food safety research workforce and the research workforce as a whole.

There is ample research showing that the foreign-born research workforce is more male dominated than the US-born research workforce in general (25). The study's analysis shows, however, that there is no difference in the proportion between foreign-born and US-born food safety researchers; the degree of female underrepresentation is similar, in terms of both their support on grants and their dissertation work.

There is a long-standing problem with data about the racial composition of the science and engineering workforce. Unfortunately, the same is true with these data – there are insufficient data to separately report detailed results about the racial composition of the workforce.[2] The research workforce in general is white and US born. About 60% of all individuals employed on research grants are white; 55% are US born. This pattern is more pronounced for USDA-funded researchers, where about 70% are white and 65% are US born. Food safety research mirrors that of research as a whole. The proportion of Asian-born researchers parallels the proportion of foreign born, accounting for approximately 60% of all foreign-born researchers. There is a distinct difference between PhD recipients in general and those receiving degrees in a food safety area. A much higher proportion of food safety PhD recipients are white, and a smaller proportion is foreign born.

6.5 Employment and Earnings Outcomes

Linkages to US Census data enable us to examine the employment and earnings outcomes of the cohort of food safety researchers and compare them both with others funded by NIH, NSF, and USDA and with the comparison. About 60% of postdoctoral researchers and graduate students are observed in US jobs one year after leaving research funding. As evident in Table 6.3, the proportion of researchers working in food safety and the comparison areas who are observed is lower than that for the research workforce as a whole. Food safety researchers who do get jobs are less likely to go into academia than their counterparts, and more likely to go into either government or the private sector.

As Figure 6.2 shows, there is a quite a complex explanation between the lower employment rate of food safety researchers. In general, as the first set

Table 6.3 *Placement of Cohort One Year after Leaving Research Funding*

	NIH, NSF, USDA	NIH	NSF	USDA	Comparison	Food Safety
Employed	59%	56%	63%	61%	53%	53%
of These:						
Academia	29%	30%	28%	35%	32%	26%
Government	6%	6%	7%	(D)	5%	7%
Private Sector	65%	64%	65%	(D)	63%	67%

Note: (D) suppressed to protect confidentiality.

[2] The Census Bureau has strict confidentiality protection rules that prohibit the release of cells with small counts.

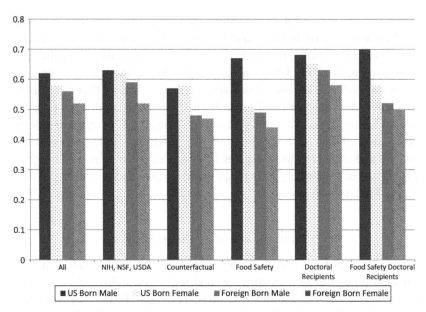

Figure 6.2 Labor force participation rate in the United States by gender and place of birth

of bars in Figure 6.2 shows, US-born researchers are more likely to be employed in the United States than are foreign born, and males are more likely to be employed than females. These findings are not surprising. Many foreign-born researchers return home (26), and women are less likely to be employed than men (8). The same pattern generally holds for all of the subgroups (NIH/NSF/USDA-funded researchers, the comparison group, and food safety researchers). However, the pattern is much stronger for food safety researchers than the other groups. So, while male, US-born food safety researchers are much more likely to be employed than the other subgroups, female, foreign-born, and female/foreign-born food safety researchers are much less likely to be employed.

The links to US Census Bureau data also permit an examination of the earnings of the research workforce. Food safety researchers generally earned less than their counterparts – their earnings one year after leaving research funding averaged just more than $46,000, compared with $58,000 for all exiters (Table 6.4). It is likely that this is due to a higher proportion of the graduate students having a master's degree as their qualification, rather than a PhD degree. The study compared their earnings with those of all others in the sector in which they were employed. When that comparison was made, it was clear that research-trained workers earned

Table 6.4 *Earnings of Analytical Sample One Year after Leaving Research Funding*

	NIH, NSF, USDA	NIH	NSF	USDA	Comparison	Food Safety
Earnings	$57,968	$51,069	$64,495	$49,594	$46,162	$46,120
Relative to Sector	1.69	1.55	1.83	1.48	1.37	1.31

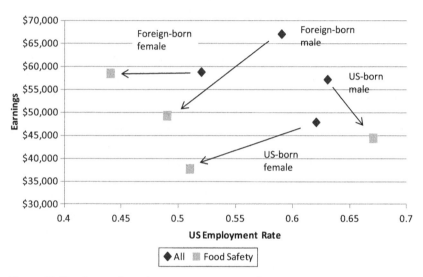

Figure 6.3 Earnings and employment rates compared

substantially more than others in the sector, although the differential is smallest for food safety researchers.

These differences in employment rates and average earnings faced by different demographic groups could affect decisions made by researchers to self-select into food safety field. As noted earlier, researchers with food safety grants and dissertations are disproportionately female compared with non-food safety research grants and dissertations. Furthermore, the degree of underrepresentation of males in food safety grants and dissertation is greater for foreign-born males than for US-born males. The earnings data can be analysed by gender and place of birth; a more complex picture then emerges about differences in earnings and employment by demographic characteristics.

Figure 6.3 compares earnings and employment differences between food safety researchers and all other researchers by demographic groups.

Table 6.5 *Earnings by Sector*

	All	NIH, NSF, USDA	Comparison	Food Safety	Doctoral Recipients All	Doctoral Recipients Food Safety
Overall	60,565	57,968	46,162	46,120	63,172	52,613
Government	64,268	65,154	41,702	44,683	70,524	78,085
Food Safety Industry	49,943	47,504	43,743	42,221	51,011	46,831

Foreign-born females in food safety research have similar earnings to their foreign-born counterparts, but are much less likely to be employed. US-born males in food safety research have higher employment rates but lower earnings than their counterparts. Both US-born female and foreign-born male food safety researchers have lower employment rates and lower earnings than other researchers in the same demographic groups.

It is also possible to analyze the differences in earnings by sector. Table 6.5 describes the earnings of the sector into which the different groups of individuals are employed. Overall, food safety–related industries do pay considerably less than other traditional research-intensive fields. Interestingly, food safety researchers entering these fields earn even less than the comparison group of overall NIH, NSF, and USDA awards. In general and for the government sector, however, food safety–trained researchers have earnings comparable to the comparison group but lower than all researchers funded by these agencies.

6.6 Summary

This initial examination suggests that the characteristics of food safety researchers are different from researchers in other fields. Faculty and staff are slightly older. The proportion of females is higher in the food safety field than in other fields, and both foreign-born females and US-born females are well represented, whereas foreign-born females suffer a greater degree of underrepresentation in other fields. The proportions of white and foreign-born researchers in the food safety field are roughly the same as those for the research workforce as a whole. Among PhD recipients, however, the proportion is higher and the proportion of foreign born is lower for PhD recipients with food safety dissertation topics compared with all PhD recipients.

Food safety researchers as a whole have slightly lower employment rates, are less likely to enter academia, and have lower earnings than researchers in other fields. US-born females have substantially lower employment rates in food safety fields than US-born males, while the employment rates for US-born females and males are comparable to those in other fields. There is an earnings premium for foreign-born female PhD recipients with food safety dissertation topics. U.S.-born females in the food safety field have a disadvantage in earnings compared with their counterparts in other fields, but no such disadvantage exists for PhD recipients with food safety dissertation topics. US-born males face a trade-off between higher earnings in nonfood safety fields and a higher employment rate in the food safety field. Foreign-born males, the most underrepresented group in food safety research, suffer from both reduced earnings and decreased employment rates when entering the food safety field.

References

[1] J. Lane, S. Bertuzzi, Measuring the Results of Science Investments. *Science* **331**, 678–680 (2011; http://science.sciencemag.org/content/331/6018/678).

[2] J. Lane, Assessing the Impact of Science Funding. *Science* **324**, 1273–1275 (2009).

[3] P. Stephan, in *Innovation Policy and the Economy*, vol. 7, J. Lerner, S. Stern, eds. (MIT Press, 2007).

[4] P. E. Stephan, *How Economics Shapes Science* (Harvard University Press, Cambridge, MA, 2012).

[5] S. T. Bell, A. J. Villado, M. A. Lukasik, L. Belau, A. L. Briggs, Getting Specific about Demographic Diversity Variable and Team Performance Relationships: A Meta-Analysis. *J. Manage.* **37**, 709–743 (2011).

[6] M. P. Feldman, D. B. Audretsch, Innovation in Cities: Science-Based Diversity, Specialization and Localized Competition. *Eur. Econ. Rev.* **43**, 409–429 (1999).

[7] D. K. Ginther et al., Race, Ethnicity, and NIH Research Awards. *Science (80-.)* **333**, 1015–1019 (2011).

[8] C. Buffington, B. C. Harris, C. Jones, B. A. Weinberg, STEM Training and Early Career Outcomes of Female and Male Graduate Students: Evidence from UMETRICS Data Linked to the 2010 Census. *Am. Econ. Rev.* **106**(5), 333–338 (2016).

[9] M. Pezzoni, J. Mairesse, P. Stephan, J. Lane, Gender and the Publication Output of Graduate Students: A Case Study. *PLoS One.* **11**, e0145146 (2016).

[10] B. Jones, B. Weinberg, Age Dynamics in Scientific Creativity. *Proceedings of the National Academy of Sciences* **108**(47), 18910–18914 (2011).

[11] F. Lissoni, J. Mairesse, F. Montobbio, M. Pezzoni, Scientific Productivity and Academic Promotion: A Study on French and Italian Physicists. *Ind. Corp. Chang.* **20**, 253–294 (2011).

[12] M. F. Fox, in *Handbook of the Sociology of Gender* (Springer, 2006), pp. 441–457.

[13] M. F. Fox, S. Mohapatra, Social-Organizational Characteristics of Work and Publication Productivity among Academic Scientists in Doctoral-Granting Departments. *J. Higher Educ.* **78**, 542–571 (2007).

[14] S. G. Levin, P. E. Stephan, Gender Differences in the Rewards to Publishing in Academe: Science in the 1970s. *Sex Roles.* **38**, 1049–1064 (1998).

[15] S. J. Ceci, D. K. Ginther, S. Kahn, W. M. Williams, Women in Academic Science: Explaining the Gap. *Psychol. Sci. Public Interes.* **15**(3), 75–141 (2014).

[16] P. A. David, *Positive Feedbacks and Research Productivity in Science: Reopening Another Black Box* (MERIT, 1993).

[17] R. K. Merton, The Matthew Effect in Science, II: Cumulative Advantage and the Symbolism of Intellectual Property. *Isis*, 606–623 (1988).

[18] P. Azoulay, C. Fons-Rosen, J. S. G. Zivin, "Does Science Advance One Funeral at a Time?" (National Bureau of Economic Research, 2015).

[19] S. P. Kerr, W. Kerr, Ç. Özden, C. Parsons, Global Talent Flows. *J. Econ. Perspect.* **30**, 83–106 (2016).

[20] C. I. Jones, Sources of US Economic Growth in a World of Ideas. *The American Economic Review* **92**(1): 220–239 (2002).

[21] S. P. Kerr, W. R. Kerr, Economic Impacts of Immigration: A Survey. *Natl. Bur. Econ. Res. Work. Pap. Ser.* **No. 16736** (2011), available at www.nber.org/papers/w16736.

[22] W. R. Kerr, W. F. Lincoln, The Supply Side of Innovation: H-1B Visa Reforms and U.S. Ethnic Invention. *J. Labor Econ.* **28**, 473–508 (2010).

[23] W. Chang, W. Chen, C. Jones, J. Lane, B. Weinberg, "Federal Funding of Doctoral Recipients Results from New Linked Survey and Transaction Data," unpublished working paper, New York University (2016).

[24] J. I. Lane, J. Owen-Smith, R. F. Rosen, B. A. Weinberg, New Linked Data on Research Investments: Scientific Workforce, Productivity, and Public Value. *Research Policy* **44**(9), 1659–1671 (2015).

[25] Grant C. Black, Paula E. Stephan, in *American Universities in a Global Market* (University of Chicago Press, 2010), pp. 129–161. Available at www.nber.org/chapters/c11595.

[26] M. Finn, "Stay Rates of Foreign Doctorate Recipients from US Universities, 2009" (Oak Ridge, TN, 2012).

New Insights into Food Safety Research Teams

Reza Sattari, Julia I. Lane, and Jason Owen-Smith

7.1 Overview

Research is done by people – and typically by people organized into research teams. In many ways, the production of science is like any business, and the principal investigator is like the CEO of a firm producing scientific ideas. This chapter examines the way in which food safety research teams are organized and how they differ from or are similar to teams in other scientific areas. The data also allow us to describe the funding sources for food safety teams. Finally, this chapter describes the nature of the networks that are formed by interactions among food safety researchers, particularly interactions among different types of researchers they work with, relative to other fields.

Understanding the productivity and effects of university research in food safety requires one to measure and characterize the structure of the teams on which the research depends. Differences in structure should matter. Most research-intensive institutions have departments and programs that cover similar arrays of topics and areas of study, and what distinguishes them from one another is not the topics they cover, but the ways in which their distinctive collaboration networks lead them to have very different scientific capabilities (1). In particular, it seems obvious that different groupings of faculty, graduate and under-graduate students, postdoctoral researchers, and staff scientists will result in very different ways in which ideas are created, transmitted, and adopted (2).

The first step is to characterize the nature of a team. This can be done in many ways; this chapter defines teams as those working on a given grant. Such an approach has a number of advantages, such as the ability to describe the proportion of graduate students and postdocs on a particular

114   *Reza Sattari, Julia I. Lane, and Jason Owen-Smith*

team and compare them with other teams. Similarly, the demographic composition of the teams can be explored, for example, the proportion who are female and the proportion who are foreign-born (3, 4). This will show how much heterogeneity there is in the "production function" of scientific activity and thus make it possible to examine the effects on scientific productivity. In the same vein, the chapter also looks at the effects of large versus small grants on team structure, noting that the National Institutes of Health has been quite vocal in asserting that $750,000 is the "optimal" size grant and that diminishing returns to scale are evident after that size (5, 6).

The second step is to describe the sources of funding. Federal research funding is complex (7). Large differences exist in the number and mix of disciplines supported by different agencies. The National Science Foundation (NSF) supports more graduate students per dollar spent than do other federal agencies. Not surprisingly, the National Institutes of Health (NIH) heavily supports biology and health PhDs, while the NSF heavily supports PhDs in engineering and mathematics. The match to ProQuest data enables one to get more insight into the funding sources and training of the subset of the sample that comprises PhD recipients. The NIH and NSF are the main direct sources of funding[1] for almost half of the PhD graduates in our data. Table 7.1 shows the large differences in the number and mix of disciplines supported by different agencies. More than 50 percent of the PhD graduates who were supported throughout entire data coverage of the UMETRICS identified "biology" or "health" as the first subject of their dissertations.[2] This pattern is quite different for PhD graduates who are funded by the NSF or US Department of Agriculture (USDA). The majority of the subjects covered in theses written by PhD students whose funding came from the NSF were "engineering" or "mathematics." Doctoral recipients supported by USDA grants wrote close to half of their theses on "agriculture" or "biology" subjects. When the sample is limited to individuals who received their degrees in 2012, one can observe similar results.

The third step is to examine research networks – or the ways in which people on different grants are connected to one another. This chapter provides an empirical analysis of research networks, including the scope

[1] Subcontract awards that could potentially be from NIH or NSF are listed as other agencies. That is because the study could not identify the source funding agency (CFDA code is stored as 00.000).
[2] ProQuest allows multiple subjects to be identified.

Table 7.1 *Subject Areas of Food Safety Dissertations by Source of Support*

NIH			NSF			USDA		
Subject	Proportion		Subject	Proportion		Subject	Proportion	
	All years	2012		All years	2012		All years	2012
Biology	38.0%	37.3%	Engineering	38.3%	34.8%	Agriculture	29.2%	39.3%
Health	18.4%	17.9%	Mathematics	11.9%	13.5%	Biology	18.8%	14.3%
Engineering	15.0%	15.3%	Biology	7.9%	7.0%	Engineering	13.9%	3.6%

and density of research connections. This analysis includes direct and indirect links among individuals through their participation in research awards, and suggests differences in the conduct and transmission of food safety research relative to other fields

7.2 Background on Teams

The importance of teams in the production of new ideas is well illustrated by the following quotation.

Silicon Valley has a regional, network-based industrial system that promotes collaborative learning and flexible adjustment among specialist producers of complex related technologies. The Region's dense social networks and open labor markets encourage experimentation and entrepreneurship. Companies compete intensely while at the same time learning from one another about changing markets and technologies through informal communication and collaborative practices ... The Route 128 region in contrast is dominated by a small number of relatively integrated companies. (8)

Just as in business, science is now done primarily by teams (9–11). The increase in the number of coauthored publications in scientific journals suggests the ongoing change in the structure of scientific research (12) – in many fields of research, coauthored articles are much more common than solo-authored ones (13–16). The pattern of authorship of scientific papers over the past 50 years shows an increase in the average number of authors per article (from 1.9 to 3.5 authors per article), which is consistent with the growth in the average size of research teams (11, 13, 14). Similar trends can be observed for patenting activity (12).

These changes in authorship patterns are common for almost all fields and disciplines. In 2010, for example, fewer than 5 percent of the papers that were published in the journal subject categories of physics, nanotechnology, and biotechnology were solo authored (17). Researchers in life and medical sciences, astronomy, and economics are also collaborating and coauthoring more (18–20).

Of course, looking at authorship alone is not a perfect way of measuring teams; such an approach ignores the role of other collaborators, including research assistants, staff, technicians, and others who may not be listed as authors on a journal article (21). As a result, the actual research team is possibly larger than what might be suggested by bibliometric data sources (22). Nevertheless, data collected from other sources (including surveys and CVs) also indicate a rapid increase in collaboration among scientists over the past decades (12, 23–25).

Many factors, including better communication technology, travel, and government interventions, may have played a role in the recent surge of research teams (*23, 26–34*). The other important factor that drives researchers toward collaboration is specialization. Increased complexity of the problems makes it very difficult for a single researcher or field to tackle scientific problems extensively (*31, 35, 36*). There is some evidence that interdisciplinary collaborations (*37, 38*) are becoming more common because scientific problems are becoming more complex and require knowledge and expertise from various disciplines (*39*). Large research teams also help to facilitate combining different perspectives and developing new notions and insights (*40, 41*). This is more obvious when scientists collaborate across fields, disciplines, and departments (*30, 42–45*).

So far, this chapter has looked only at the advantages of research teams. Similar to any collaborative enterprise, scientific teams incur significant transaction costs (*12*). Researchers need to deal with geographical and cultural diversities, despite improved ways of communication (*46*). The transaction cost may vary from one type of collaboration to another. For example, Bikard et al. (2015) find that cross-departmental research taking place within the same university is actually less costly than that across different universities. However, the coordination costs are more of an issue when the collaboration is extended over disciplines and involves researchers from multiple universities (*32, 47*). Moreover, young scholars in early stages of their career are more prone to communication and coordination costs. One reason for this could be that they are more likely to be involved in interdisciplinary research (*48*).

Large initiatives also vary with respect to the collaborative orientations and disciplinary perspectives of team members (*49*). Stokols et al. offer the following overview of different levels of disciplinarity:

- Intradisciplinary: working within a single discipline
- Cross-disciplinary: viewing one discipline from the perspective of another
- Multidisciplinary: people from different disciplines working together, each drawing on their disciplinary knowledge
- Interdisciplinary: integrating knowledge and methods from different disciplines, using a real synthesis of approaches
- Transdisciplinary: creating a unity of intellectual frameworks beyond the disciplinary perspectives. (*51*)

There are no clear distinctions between cross-disciplinary and unidisciplinary collaborations, but definition of individual disciplines and level of integration play an important role in determining this difference (52). To define discipline, Stokols et al. write:

Disciplines are generally organized around distinctive substantive interests (e.g., biological, psychological, environmental, or sociologic phenomena); analytic levels (e.g., molecular, cellular, cognitive, behavioral, interpersonal, organizational, community); and concepts, methods, and measures associated with particular fields. The boundaries between disciplines and sub-disciplines are to some extent arbitrarily defined and agreed upon by communities of scholars. For instance, the boundaries between some fields may be overlapping (e.g., physiology and molecular biology) and other fields, such as public health and urban planning, are inherently multidisciplinary in that they combine several disciplinary perspectives in analyses of population health and urban development. (51)

The complex nature of team science, therefore, requires deeper analysis of this subject. Analysis of team studies are in general done at three levels: micro-, meso-, and macro levels. Population-level analyses that study the patterns of collaboration in general terms and analyze the fields of knowledge and their integration are within the range of macro-level analysis (53). The most common tool for this approach is network analysis of the collaboration across disciplines (54, 55). Meso-level analyses focus on research groups and study the dynamics of collaboration within science teams (56). This approach is centered around the evolution and the influence of various network measures over time (57, 58). Micro-level studies, on the other hand, are interested in analyzing individual members of researcher teams and try to understand the role of various individual characteristics and interventions on specific individual outcomes (59–61).

Network theory is a particularly attractive approach. Researchers have studied the effect of importance of researchers to their network and their position on consequent outcomes and performance of the teams and individuals (62, 63). Several studies find a strong relationship between different measures of network centrality and higher levels of innovation and team productivity (64–66).

There are three general indicators of a node's centrality in a network: *betweenness, closeness,* and *degree centrality* (67–70). Betweenness centrality is equal to the number of shortest paths from all vertices to all others that include that node. A node with high betweenness centrality has a large influence on the transfer of information and knowledge through the network, under the assumption that item transfer follows the shortest paths. The closeness centrality (or closeness) of a node indicates how long it will take to spread information from that node to all other nodes sequentially. It is calculated as the sum of the lengths of the shortest paths between the node and all other nodes in a network. Thus the more central a node is, the closer it is to all the other nodes; it might serve as an information hub or a reference point for other members of the network. Degree centrality is another highly effective measure of the importance or influence of a node. It is calculated as the number of edges incident to the node, and it is similar to closeness centrality (71, 72).

7.3 Some Basic Facts

UMETRICS data enable one, for the first time, to describe the number and types of projects worked on by a typical principal investigator in the food safety research area, as well as the size and composition of the principal investigator's research teams. The data are complex, so there are many ways to capture the participation of individuals on grants. Table 7.2 shows summary information about the different ways that grant support can be captured across individuals and time. The first panel provides general

Table 7.2 *Awards and Individuals Paid on Awards by Year*

	Panel 1:			Panel 2: Unique Individuals Sample Occupation – Duration Restricted		
Year	Unique Awards	Unique Individuals	Unique Individuals × Award	All	Food Safety	Food Safety Comparison
2001	2,530	8,807	12,718	2,743	111	153
2002	3,094	11,107	17,178	3,474	132	185
2003	3,364	11,775	18,293	3,649	146	233
2004	4,820	16,820	27,470	4,734	186	402
2005	6,310	17,400	31,002	4,541	195	389
2006	7,304	18,167	33,408	5,142	239	480
2007	13,986	32,629	58,311	8,081	427	811
2008	19,229	43,123	82,741	11,949	656	1,105
2009	21,979	49,924	95,242	14,923	894	1,516
2010	25,950	62,954	121,030	18,182	1,198	1,823
2011	27,553	70,314	132,982	20,972	1,208	1,990
2012	31,302	77,582	147,208	23,138	1,322	2,176
2013	38,384	96,671	193,977	25,493	1,313	2,392
2014	45,078	111,076	210,785	33,194	1,509	2,880
2015	38,413	97,049	176,409	25,489	1,182	2,143
2016	9,830	26,239	43,014	5,748	277	449

information about the sample as a whole; the second focuses on providing information about the research population of interest for this study.

The first column in the first panel in Table 7.2 provides information (repeated from Chapter 5) about the awards by year in UMETRICS. Note that although there are a total of about 300,000 award-years, there are 120,958 unique awards since many awards span multiple years. After excluding training awards and awards made to small businesses, 117,150 remain. Around 33,768 awards have been topic modeled and are either flagged as "food safety" or "nonfood safety." Note that the count for each year varies, because of the different ranges of data provided by each participating university. Because most universities reported data in 2012, in much of the following the results are for the entire sample and for 2012.

The second column in Table 7.2 shows the individuals supported by each award. Close to 270,000 unique individuals have been paid by these awards. Of course, individuals can be funded over multiple years; there are 751,637 such individual-by-year observations.

To see the connections between individuals and awards in each year, one can also choose the unit of observation as individual by award by year. Column 3 of Table 7.2 provides information on that particular slice of the data. There are 1,401,768 individuals by award by year; this approach can count individuals multiple times – one for each award in each year.

The second panel of Table 7.2 contains information about the focus of the study, individuals who are substantively involved in research. Since the UMETRICS data include information by occupation, as well as the length of time that awardees are on grant funding, the last triplet of columns indicated as panel 2 in the table provides counts of unique individuals that are limited to specific occupations (faculty graduate students and postdoctoral researchers). The sample is further restricted by excluding graduate students and postdoctoral researchers from an award in a given year if they are paid for fewer than 6 months on that award in that year. The first column provides counts of all such individuals for each year. The second column provides counts of those in food safety research; the final column provides the same information for food safety comparisons (defined in earlier chapters).

7.4 Describing Teams

7.4.1 Team Size

Team size is a standard way of measuring the degree to which researchers collaborate. The measure of team size for a publication is straightforward; it is simply the number of coauthors. It is more complex with these data, because grants span multiple time periods, and researchers can be funded on multiple awards. Indeed, as Table 7.3 demonstrates, in any given year, the average individual working on food safety grants is funded on about three awards. If everyone is included who was ever paid on a grant as a team member in each year, the average team size for food safety grantees will be as high as 62. However, if a team is composed only of researchers (faculty, graduate students, and postdocs), the average team size drops to 26.75 for food safety researchers. In all cases, food safety researchers work on larger teams than their counterparts.

Team size for each researcher (faculty members plus postdoc and graduate students, who are paid for at least six months on a grant in that year) is calculated. The connectedness measure is defined as the number of other nodes connected directly to an individual (which is equal to the degree centrality of that node) plus one (to include the individuals themselves). Compared with their counterparts, food safety teams are more likely to be connected to more than 10 other researchers.

This difference in team size between the two groups does not seem to be driven as a result of differences in grant length or size. As apparent in Tables 7.4 and 7.5, there are no systematic differences in terms of grant size and/or project length between the two groups of researchers. One potential explanation, aside from the fact that food safety researchers on average have slightly more grants, could be that the problems that both groups face

Table 7.3 *Team Size Calculations under Alternative Team Definitions*

Group	Average Number of Awards for All Individuals		Average Number of People on Main Award		Average Number of People on Other Awards	
	All	Researchers	All	Researchers	All	Researchers
Food Safety	2.46	3.09	35.17	11.75	62.22	26.75
Comparison	2.15	2.66	15.2	6.37	34.26	17.24

Table 7.4 *Obligated Grant Size by Research Topic*

Obligated Amount	Food Safety	Comparison Group
0–100K	10%	12%
100K–250K	25%	22%
250K–1 mil	56%	56%
> 1 mil	9%	10%

Table 7.5 *Project Length by Research Topic*

Project Length	Food Safety	Comparison Group
1 year or less	17%	0.16
2 years	31%	0.34
3 years	20%	0.18
4 years	16%	0.15
5 years or more	16%	0.17

are more complex and interdisciplinary. However, there is no direct way of testing this hypothesis.

This finding holds true even if the sample is reduced to include the most highly refined measure – researchers (faculty, graduate students, and postdocs) who are funded for at least six months. If team size is calculated for every given year for this group, team size is greater for food safety researchers both for all teams and for the comparison group.

7.4.2 Network Centrality

The standard measures of centrality in the context of grants are relatively straightforward to calculate. In this analysis, when two researchers (nodes) are connected if they are paid on the same grant, degree centrality shows how many other researchers are being paid on the same grants as an individual has in each year. So, for example, if a researcher is supported by two grants in 2012, and there are four distinct other researchers on each of those awards, then this researcher has eight direct ties in 2012. As a reminder, closeness centrality is defined as the sum of the lengths of the shortest paths between the node and all other nodes in a network, and central nodes are closer to all other nodes.

For each researcher, the betweenness measure is equal to the number of shortest paths from each vertex to all others that include that researcher. Thus, a node with high betweenness centrality has a large influence on the transfer of information and knowledge through the network, under the assumption that item transfer follows the shortest paths.

In the next step, the network of individuals and awards will be constructed and some network measures estimated for each individual in each year. Before doing so, note that the UMETRICS employee data set is a two-mode network because it represents relationships between two different classes of nodes, grants, and people. To use data of this form to address

Table 7.6 *Network Centrality Measures*

	All Unique Ind × Year	Ever Food Safety	Never Food Safety	Ever Comparison – Never Food Safety
Degree	15.50	20.11	15.25	12.22
Closeness (×10,000)	7.88	8.22	7.87	7.77
Betweenness (×10,000)	4.47	12.6	4.03	7.13
Obs(indXyr)	211,231	10,995	200,455	19,127

questions about patterns of collaboration among researchers, one must first transform the network to represent collaborative relationships.[3]

A person-by-person projection of the original bipartite network assumes that ties exist between people when they are paid by the same grant. Similarly, a grant-by-grant projection of the original two-mode network assumes that ties exist between grants when they pay the same people. In other words, two nodes (individuals) are connected to each other in a given year, if they are paid on the same grant that year.

Table 7.6 provides a summary of various network centrality measures across all years for all the researchers who satisfy duration restrictions and are paid on any award in UMETRICS (federal and nonfederal) that are not excluded. Food safety researchers have much higher (normalized) betweenness centrality compared with nonfood safety researchers and those who are flagged as being in the comparison group (12.6 vs. 7.13), implying that food safety researchers are in a better position to broker and thus might have better opportunities for innovation. The results for closeness centrality are also consistent with the betweenness centrality measures and suggest that food safety researchers are more central. However, the difference in terms of closeness centrality between food safety researchers and their counterparts is quite small (8.22 vs. 7.77) and estimated with much noise.

7.5 Summary

This chapter has provided some sense of how the new UMETRICS data can be used to describe the complexity of research in general and food

---

[3] For this transformation, the study used the *igraph* package in R to construct two separate one-mode projections (person × person, and grant × grant) of the original two-mode or bipartite (grant × person) network.

safety research in particular. While previous "science of science" policy literature has focused almost exclusively on the activities of either principal investigators or authors, this chapter describes the full structure of research teams. It also provides more information on how food safety researchers collaborate with researchers working on other grants.

Much more can be done. In particular, future work could examine why food safety researchers work in larger teams and are more connected. It could examine the role of institutional structures such as centers, as well as the importance of the interdisciplinary nature of food safety research in pulling in researchers from different fields. It could also exploit differences in university structures – particularly whether a university has a medical school or is a land grant non medical school – to get a better understanding of how related funding activities affect the composition of food safety research teams.

References

[1]   J. Owen-Smith, in *Big Data and Social Science*, I. Foster, R. Ghani, R. Jarmin, F. Kreuter, J. Lane, eds. (Taylor & Francis, 2016).

[2]   B. A. Weinberg et al., Science Funding and Short-Term Economic Activity. *Science* **344**, 41–43 (2014).

[3]   C. Buffington, B. C. Harris, C. Jones, B. A. Weinberg, STEM Training and Early Career Outcomes of Female and Male Graduate Students: Evidence from UMETRICS Data Linked to the 2010 Census. *Am. Eco. Rev.* **106** (5), 333–338. (2016).

[4]   M. Pezzoni, J. Mairesse, P. Stephan, J. Lane, Gender and the Publication Output of Graduate Students: A Case Study. *PLoS One* **11**, e0145146 (2016).

[5]   J. R. Lorsch, Maximizing the Return on Taxpayers' Investments in Fundamental Biomedical Research. *Mol. Biol. Cell.* **26**, 1578–1582 (2015).

[6]   J. Berg, Estimated Publication Outputs as a Function of Number of R01 Grants per PI. *Datahound Blog* (2015), available at http://datahound.scientopia.

[7]   W. Chang, W. Chen, C. Jones, J. Lane, B. Weinberg, "Federal Funding of Doctoral Recipients Results from New Linked Survey and Transaction Data." No. w23019. *National Bureau of Economic Research* (2017).

[8]   A. Saxenian, *Regional Networks: Industrial Adaptation in Silicon Valley and Route 128* (Cambridge: Harvard University Press, 1994).

[9]   K. Hwang, International Collaboration in Multilayered Center-Periphery in the Globalization of Science and Technology. *Sci. Technol. Hum. Values* **33** (1), 101–133 (2008).

[10] T. Luukkonen, O. Persson, G. Siverstsen, Understanding Patterns of International Scientific Collaboration. *Sci. Technol. Hum. Values.* **17**, 101–126 (1992).

[11] S. Wuchty, B. F. Jones, B. Uzzi, The Increasing Dominance of Teams in Production of Knowledge. *Plant Cell.* **316**, 2005–2008 (2007).

[12] T. L. O'Brien, Change in Academic Coauthorship, 1953–2003. *Sci. Technol. Hum. Values.* **37**, 210–234 (2012).

[13] J. D. Adams, G. C. Black, J. R. Clemmons, P. E. Stephan, Scientific Teams and Institutional Collaborations: Evidence from U.S. Universities, 1981–1999. *Res. Policy.* **34**, 259–285 (2005).

[14] J. A. Fernandez, The Transition from an Individual Science to a Collective One: The Case of Astronomy. *Scientometrics.* **42**, 61–74 (1998).

[15] W. M. Lee, Publication Trends of Doctoral Students in Three Fields from 1965–1995. *J. Am. Soc. Inf. Sci. Technol.* **51**, 139–144 (2000).

[16] M. E. J. Newman, Coauthorship Networks and Patterns of Scientific Collaboration. *Proc. Natl. Acad. Sci. U. S. A.* **101 Suppl.**, 5200–5205 (2004).

[17] R. B. Freeman, I. Ganguli, R. Murciano-Goroff, Why and Wherefore of Increased Scientific Collaboration. *The Changing Frontier: Rethinking Science and Innovation Policy* **17** (2015).

[18] J. Parker, B. Penders, N. Vermeulen, *Collaboration in the New Life Sciences* (Routledge, 2016).

[19] J. Hudson, Trends in Multi-authored Papers in Economics. *J. Econ. Perspect.* **10**, 153–158 (1996).

[20] S. Milojević, Principles of Scientific Research Team Formation and Evolution. *Proc. Natl. Acad. Sci. U. S. A.* **111**, 3984–3989 (2014).

[21] J. M. Lewis, S. Ross, T. Holden, The How and Why of Academic Collaboration: Disciplinary Differences and Policy Implications. *High. Educ.* **64**, 693–708 (2012).

[22] E. Leahey, From Sole Investigator to Team Scientist: Trends in the Practice and Study of Research Collaboration. *Annu. Rev. Sociol.* **42**, 81–100 (2016).

[23] E. B. Araujo, A. A. Moreira, V. Furtado, T. H. C. Pequeno, J. S. Andrade, Collaboration Networks from a Large CV Database: Dynamics, Topology and Bonus Impact. *PLoS One* **9**, 1–7 (2014).

[24] B. Bozeman, E. Corley, Scientists' Collaboration Strategies: Implications for Scientific and Technical Human Capital. *Res. Policy.* **33**, 599–616 (2004).

[25] P. C. Boardmana, E. A. Corley, University Research Centers and the Composition of Research Collaborations. *Res. Policy.* **37**, 900–913 (2008).

[26] G. Melin, Pragmatism and Self-Organization. *Res. Policy.* **29**, 31–40 (2000).

[27] L. Dahlander, D. A. McFarland, Ties That Last: Tie Formation and Persistence in Research Collaborations over Time. *Adm. Sci. Q.* **58**, 69–110 (2013).

[28] M. Binz-Scharf, Y. Kalish, L. Paik, Making Science New Generations of Collaborative Knowledge Production. *Am. Behav. Sci.* **59** (5), 531–547. (2015).

[29] J. S. Katz, B. R. Martin, What Is Research Collaboration? *Res. Policy.* **26**, 1–18 (1997).

[30] M. A. Bikard, F. E. Murray, J. S. Gans, Exploring Tradeoffs in the Organization of Scientific Work: Collaboration and Scientific Reward. *Manage. Sci.* **61**, 1473–1495 (2015).

[31] B. Y. Clark, J. J. Llorens, Investments in Scientific Research: Examining the Funding Threshold Effects on Scientific Collaboration and Variation by Academic Discipline. *Policy Stud. J.* **40**, 698–729 (2012).

[32] J. N. Cummings, S. Kiesler, Coordination Costs and Project Outcomes in Multi-University Collaborations. *Res. Policy.* **36**, 1620–1634 (2007).

[33] C. M. Rawlings, D. A. McFarland, L. Dahlander, D. Wang, Streams of Thought: Knowledge Flows and Intellectual Cohesion in a Multidisciplinary Era. *Soc. Forces.* **93**, 1687–1722 (2015).

[34]   D. J. de Solla Price, *Little Science, Big Science, and Beyond* (New York: Columbia University Press, 1986).

[35]   J. A. Evans, Electronic Publication and the Narrowing of Science and Scholarship. *Science* **321**, 395–399 (2008).

[36]   B. F. Jones, S. Wuchty, B. Uzzi, Multi-University Research Teams: Shifting Impact, Geography, and Stratification in Science. *Science*. **322**, 1259–1262 (2008).

[37]   W. F. Boh, Y. Ren, S. Kiesler, R. Bussjaeger, Expertise and Collaboration in the Geographically Dispersed Organization. *Organ. Sci.* **18**, 595–612 (2007).

[38]   K. B. Wray, Rethinking Scientific Specialization. *Soc. Stud. Sci.* **35**, 151–164 (2005).

[39]   M. L. Bennett, H. Gadlin, Collaboration and Team Science: From Theory to Practice. *J. Investig. Med.* **60**, 768–775 (2012).

[40]   J. R. Hackman, Why Teams Don't Work, in *Theory and Research on Small Groups*, R. S. Tindale et al., eds., pp. 245–267 (New York: Plenum, 1998)

[41]   J. R. Hackman, *Collaborative Intelligence: Using Teams to Solve Hard Problems* (Berrett-Koehler, 2011).

[42]   E. Leahey, J. Moody, Sociological Innovation through Subfield Integration. *Soc. Curr.* **1**, 228–256 (2014).

[43]   E. Leahey, C. M. Beckman, T. L. Stanko, Prominent but Less Productive: The Impact of Interdisciplinarity on Scientists' Research. *Administrative Science Quarterly* **62** (1), 105–139 (2017)..

[44]   V. Larivière, S. Haustein, K. Börner, Long-Distance Interdisciplinarity Leads to Higher Scientific Impact. *PLoS One* **10**, 1–15 (2015).

[45]   B. Uzzi, S. Mukherjee, M. Stringer, B. Jones, Atypical Combinations and Scientific Impact. *Science* **342**, 468–472 (2013).

[46]   J. P. Walsh, N. G. Maloney, Collaboration Structure, Communication Media, and Problems in Scientific Work Teams. *J. Comput. Commun.* **12**, 378–398 (2007).

[47]   J. N. Cummings, S. Kiesler, Collaborative Research across Disciplinary and Organizational Boundaries. *Soc. Stud. Sci.* **35**, 703–722 (2005).

[48]   D. Rhoten, A. Parker, Education: Risks and Rewards of an Interdisciplinary Research Path. *Science (80-.)* **306**, 2046 (2004).

[49]   D. Stokols, S. Misra, R. P. Moser, K. L. Hall, B. K. Taylor, The Ecology of Team Science: Understanding Contextual Influences on Transdisciplinary Collaboration. *Am. J. Prev. Med.* **305** (2008), doi:10.1016/j.amepre.2008.05.003.

[50]   M. Stember, Advancing the Social Sciences through the Interdisciplinary Enterprise. *Soc. Sci. J.* **28**, 1–14 (1991).

[51]   D. Stokols, K. L. Hall, B. K. Taylor, R. P. Moser, The Science of Team Science: Overview of the Field and Introduction to the Supplement. *Am. J. Prev. Med.* **35** (2008), doi:10.1016/j.amepre.2008.05.002.

[52]   P. Weingart, N. Stehr, eds., *Practising Interdisciplinarity* (Toronto: University of Toronto Press, 2000).

[53]   H. J. Falk-Krzesinski et al., Mapping a Research Agenda for the Science of Team Science. *Res. Eval.* **20**, 145–158 (2011).

[54]   S. W. Aboelela, J. Merrill, K. M. Carley, E. Larson, Social Network Analysis to Evaluate an Interdisciplinary Research Center. *J. Res. Adm.* **38**, 61–79 (2007).

[55] V. A. Haines, J. Godley, P. Hawe, Understanding Interdisciplinary Collaborations as Social Networks. *Am. J. Community Psychol.* **47**, 1–11 (2011).

[56] S. M. Fiore, Interdisciplinarity as Teamwork: How the Science of Teams Can Inform Team Science. *Small Gr. Res.* **39**, 251–277 (2008).

[57] J. Keyton, D. J. Ford, F. L. Smith, A Mesolevel Communicative Model of Collaboration. *Commun. Theory.* **18**, 376–406 (2008).

[58] K. Börner et al., A Multi-Level Systems Perspective for the Science of Team Science. *Sci. Transl. Med.* **2** (2010), doi:10.1126/scitranslmed.3001399.A.

[59] M. Borrego, L. Newswander, Definitions of Interdisciplinary Research: Toward Graduate-Level Interdisciplinary Learning Outcomes. *Rev. High. Educ.* **34**, 61–84 (2010).

[60] M. Mitrany, Gauging the Transdisciplinary Qualities and Outcomes of Doctoral Training Programs. *J. Plan. Educ. Res.* **24**, 437–449 (2005).

[61] J. M. Nash, Transdisciplinary Training: Key Components and Prerequisites for Success. *Am. J. Prev. Med.* **35** (2008), doi:10.1016/j.amepre.2008.05.004.

[62] M. Granovetter, Economic Action and Social Structure: The Problem of Embeddedness. *Am. J. Sociol.* **91**, 481–510 (1985).

[63] B. Uzzi, Social Structure and Competition in Interfirm Networks: The Paradox of Embeddedness. *Adm. Sci. Q.* **42**, 35–67 (1997).

[64] J. Owen-Smith, W. W. Powell, Knowledge Networks as Channels and Conduits: The Effects of Spillovers in the Boston Biotechnology Community. *Organ. Sci.* **15**, 5–21 (2004).

[65] R. Grewal, G. L. Lilien, G. Mallapragada, Location, Location, Location: How Network Embeddedness Affects Project Success in Open Source Systems. *Manage. Sci.* **52**, 1043–1056 (2006).

[66] P. V. Singh, Y. Tan, V. Mookerjee, Network Effects: The Influence of Structural Capital on Open Source Project Success. *MIS Q.* **35**, 813–829 (2011).

[67] G. Sabidussi, The Centrality of a Graph. *Psychometrika.* **31**, 581–603 (1966).

[68] R. S. Burt, *Structural Holes: The Social Structure of Competition* (Harvard University Press, 2009).

[69] L. C. Freeman, A Set of Measures of Centrality Based on Betweenness. *Sociometry* **40**, 35–41 (1977).

[70] J. M. Anthonissen, *The Rush in a Directed Graph* (Amsterdam: SMC, 1971).

[71] S. Wasserman, K. Faust, *Social Network Analysis: Methods and Applications.* (Cambridge, UK, and New York: Cambridge University Press, 1994).

[72] B. Stvilia et al., Composition of Scientific Teams and Publication Productivity at a National Science Lab. *J. Am. Soc. Inf. Sci. Technol.* **62**, 270–283 (2011).

8

Assessing the Effects of Food Safety Research on Early Career Outcomes

John L. King, Stanley R. Johnson, and Matthew B. Ross

8.1 Introduction

The impact of a research award includes not just scientific discoveries and publications, but also the training and experience gained by early career researchers. As Oppenheimer pointed out, the best way to send knowledge is to wrap it up in a human being (1). Indeed, the abundant regional economic activity surrounding universities strongly suggests that regionally bound human beings, not globally accessible documents, are the key to understanding economic impact. As noted in Chapter 3, the conceptual framework is straightforward. Undergraduate students, graduate students, and postdoctoral researchers taking part in scientific projects obtain valuable training while at the same time creating new knowledge that can be transmitted to their employers once their training is complete. The benefits that result from their application of knowledge gained through research training accrue to both the employing firm and the workers. Researchers create new ideas that either directly generate new businesses or are transmitted through social and scientific networks to the private sector.

Subsequent chapters describe discoveries in food safety research as measured by patents and publications. This chapter focuses on the aspect of the transmission of knowledge as measured by the early career outcomes of graduate students and postdoctoral scholars who participate in federal research awards. Observing differences in early career outcomes such as employment and earnings provides some initial evidence about the pathways of research impact closely associated with these individuals.

This chapter reports on the labor market outcomes of early career researchers in food safety following participation in federally sponsored research. In particular, it highlights two kinds of outcomes: (1) employment outcomes, both overall and sector-specific employment and

(2) earnings. In keeping with the earlier chapters, their outcomes are compared with a reasonable comparison group.

8.2 Background

There is an extensive literature linking agricultural research with increases in agricultural productivity, starting with Griliches's classic analysis of hybrid corn adoption and continuing to general equilibrium analysis that incorporates temporal, spatial, and crop-specific dimensions (2–4). These approaches depend on mostly complete characterizations of inputs and outputs and are usually limited to commodity agriculture. To address market externalities, Fernandez-Cornejo et al. incorporate pesticide toxicity data into price and quantity indices used in the productivity analysis, and other studies and have included environmental externalities such as climate change and water quality (5, 6). However, food safety externalities have not been linked in this agricultural productivity literature, partly due to the difficulty of characterizing inputs and outputs (7). Even the detailed and comprehensive analysis of trends in private and public agricultural research provided by Fuglie et al. does not characterize food safety investments as a separate category of research (8). This book contributes both new data on food safety research and new models to complement the analysis of research impacts in food and agriculture.

Beyond research in the food and agricultural sectors, the broader literature on innovation documents links between research funding and outputs such as patents and publication. For instance, Sampat provides a very careful overview, particularly with respect to the biomedical literature (9). However, lack of data on the direct links between changes in research funding and the research workforce – particularly at the margin in terms of the effect of training new doctoral students – means that the impact has not been studied in the United States. Indeed, because there are many different sources of federal funding, and each agency has access only to its own data, it has not been possible to capture how agency funding is interconnected at either the faculty or the individual student level. As Freeman notes, there is a desperate need for data to "understand the market dynamics that govern the response of the job market to changes in government policies" (10).

The linking mechanism is well understood in theory – increased funding in a particular field supports more principal investigators, and they, in turn, train graduate students in the process of doing their research. However, empirically tracing the link is difficult (1, 11). Waldinger has made clever use of exogenous shocks associated with both Nazi Germany and Russian policies to examine the link between research and production of new scientists (*12, 13*). Stephan, in a series of papers and a recent book, has pointed out that relative salaries, the availability of financial support, and demographic factors affect the production of PhDs (*14, 15*). Freeman and Van Reenan show that labor markets for early career scientists are a constraint on the growth of scientific discoveries even (or especially) during a recent period of rapid National Institutes of Health (NIH) funding growth (*16*).

Some research on doctoral recipients has been done using UMETRICS data (*1, 17*), which, because it is drawn directly from payroll records for a subset of universities, makes it possible to identify the entire constellation of research teams engaged conducting research, including faculty, under-graduate and graduate students, postdocs, and staff. The UMETRICS data have been linked to US Census placement and Web of Science data to document the employment and earnings outcomes of graduate students employed on projects, including gender differences (*18, 19*). That work described the major sectors into which doctoral recipients formerly on research payrolls and in the sample flowed in the year subsequent to their separation from university employment. The majority go to academia – presumably many to postdoctoral or faculty positions. A large percentage get jobs in industry; notably about 21 percent in R&D-intensive firms (relative to 5.3 percent in the United States as a whole) and about 21.6 percent in non-R&D-intensive firms (vs. 81 percent in the United States as a whole). Only a small percentage entered government, although this is at a higher level than the United States as a whole. The employers are much more likely to be in high-skill industries such as engineering, high-tech, and professional service fields (including medicine) than US employers at large. For example, the shares of doctoral recipients employed in pharma-ceutical and medicine manufacturing and computer systems design are more than six times the US average. At the other end of the spectrum, uncommon employment destinations for doctoral recipients are grocery stores and limited-service eating places.

8.3 Data

This chapter focuses on the early earnings and employment outcomes of graduate students and postdoctoral researchers. For early career faculty, participation in federally funded research might also have dramatic effects on eventual career outcomes, but these effects can occur over longer time periods and depend on other factors (*3*, *4*, *5*). By contrast, there is a reasonable expectation that graduate students and postdoctoral scholars who participate in federally sponsored research are linked more strongly to the topic of the research, and that their first jobs after separating from their respective universities are related to that experience. The analysis here excludes undergraduate students. Although the same effects can be present for undergraduate students who participate in research (*1*, *2*), there is not as strong a link between this experience and immediate post-undergraduate employment or eventual career outcomes.

As discussed in detail in Chapter 5, the study developed a comparison group consisting of individuals funded by any USDA award or NIH and NSF programs where a large portion of the total awards was identified as food safety. Although the study's empirical analysis presents results comparing food safety researchers with the overall analytical sample, the focus is on the results relative to the aforementioned comparison group, because it further restricts the sample to individuals working on research similar to food safety and whose early career outcomes are also presumably similar. Comparing all NIH grants with NIH food safety grants is obviously not sensible, because the NIH funds both basic and applied research that in content and structure is very different from food safety research. Similarly, the NSF funds food safety research but also funds engineering, astrophysics, and computer science. A comparison between researchers funded by food safety awards and those on dissimilar NSF and NIH awards is inappropriate, as early career outcomes vary largely from inherent structural differences across the career pathways in these fields.

In the development of the comparison group, the study first identified (through the text analysis approach described in Chapter 4) both food safety grants and grants that are "nonfood safety." Also identified were all grants associated with each funding program – NSF, NIH, and USDA. "Food safety funding programs" can then be characterized in two ways: (1) those that have funded at least one award that is food safety (called "food safety funding program") and (2) those that have at least 5 percent of their funding portfolio in food safety (called "intense food safety funding program"). The study then identified three possible comparison groups. One comprised is grants that were funded by the USDA that are "not food safety." The second comprised grants that were "not food safety" in a food safety funding program. The third comprised grants that were "not food safety" in an "intense food safety funding program."

The last group, intense food safety funding programs, is combined here with all nonfood safety awards made by USDA and referred to in this chapter as the comparison group. There were 120 programs where the abstract of at least one award was available. As noted, this comparison group included only researchers who were never funded on a food safety award, but were funded by USDA or on a nonfood safety award from an NIH or NSF program where greater than 5 percent of the total awards in UMETRICS were identified as food safety (see Appendix 5.2 in Chapter 5). The eligible programs included Biological Sciences at NSF (8 percent food safety) and NIH awards from Microbiology and Infectious Diseases Research (7 percent food safety), Allergy and Infectious Diseases Research (10 percent), Human Genome Research (11 percent), Environmental Health (12 percent), Occupational Safety and Health (15 percent), Food and Drug Administration Research (44 percent), and National Institute of Environmental Health Sciences (NIEHS) Superfund Hazardous Substances Basic Research (56 percent).

Due to the combination of both UMETRICS and US Census data, it is now possible to retroactively generate multiple comparison groups of individuals. The study first developed an analytical sample consisting of graduate students and postdoctoral researchers (as discussed in detail in Chapter 6). Specifically, the study examined only those who had the possibility of being observed in a research award transaction for the 24 months prior to separation from the university.[1] This group is called the "analytical sample" in previous chapters, and the workforce outcomes and training environment of this group are examined relative to the comparison groups.

In this chapter, the UMETRICS data were matched with Census data including the Longitudinal Employer-Household Dynamics (LEHD), Decennial Census, American Community Survey, and W-2 earnings records, as described in Chapter 3. A separate analysis was also done for doctoral recipients, as a result of matching the data to ProQuest dissertation abstracts (also described in Chapter 3). While the main outcomes of interest are employment, earnings, and completing a dissertation, the richness of the data permits a somewhat deeper analysis in two

---

[1]   Earnings and employment data extend to 2015, so only those individuals were examined whose last observation in UMETRICS was either on or before 2013 or two years after their university began reporting data. The end date of 2013 was set so that the study would have at least one year of available earnings data to examine short-term workforce outcomes.

dimensions. The first is whether or not the individual in question got a job in a food safety–related industry. After consultation with experts and reviewing the data, the study classified a food safety–related industry as food production (agriculture), food distribution (industries associated with distributing food), and food retail (industries associated with selling food). The second is the production of a dissertation related to food safety: The application of text analysis to dissertation abstracts permits such an analysis.

There were 443 food safety researchers in the analytical sample as compared with 7,884 total nonfood safety researchers, of which 1,043 were from the comparison group. Of the analytical sample, 250 food safety researchers were matched to the combined Census data as compared with 5,000 nonfood safety researchers, of which 600 were from the comparison group. Based on very high labor-force participation and employment rates for demographically similar individuals, the majority of individuals unmatched to Census administrative records – those who show up as not employed – were likely to have returned to their country of origin after completing graduate studies (*20*).

8.4 Descriptive Statistics of Early Career Food Safety Researchers

Table 8.1 displays the basic demographics and award characteristics for the food safety researchers relative to the overall analytical sample and comparison group. As shown in Table 8.1, early career food safety researchers are 55 percent female compared with 41 percent for the entire analytical sample and 47 percent in the comparison group. The estimates of employment and wage outcomes presented later in this chapter control for greater female composition of early career food safety researchers in light of generally lower labor market earnings for females (*7*). Food safety researchers are more likely to be US born than the overall analytical group, but less likely relative to the comparison group. Of the last 24 months an individual was observed in the sample, food safety researchers were observed to have been funded for a substantially longer period of time relative to both other groups. Although food safety individuals were defined as those ever having been on such an award, and nonfood safety individuals as those who have not, the bottommost panel of Table 8.1 shows the crossover of funding for individuals from each group.

Table 8.2 presents descriptive statistics pertaining to early career outcomes of the different cohorts using the match of UMETRICS data to US

Table 8.1 *Demographic Characteristics of Analytical Sample*

			Analytical Sample			
				Funding Source		
		All	Nonfood Safety	Comparison	Food Safety	Doctoral Recipients
Sample Size		9,400	5,000	600	250	4,000
Average Age		32	32	33	33	31
Gender	Male	62%	59%	53%	45%	66%
	Female	38%	41%	47%	55%	34%
Race	White	62%	60%	67%	62%	56%
	Black or African American	4%	4%	N/A	N/A	4%
	Asian	31%	33%	27%	31%	38%
	Other Race	3%	3%	N/A	N/A	3%
Ethnicity	Hispanic	6%	6%	7%	4%	5%
	Non-Hispanic	94%	94%	93%	96%	95%
Place of Birth	US Born	55%	54%	60%	56%	49%
	Asian Born	27%	29%	24%	26%	34%
	Western Europe and Canada Born	7%	7%	6%	7%	6%
	Other Place Born	11%	10%	10%	11%	10%
Award	Funded Days	632	655	666	697	619
Award Topic	All Nonfood Safety	53%	100%	100%	—	56%
	NIH Nonfood Safety	27%	50%	48%	—	24%
	NSF Nonfood Safety	27%	51%	38%	—	33%
	USDA Nonfood Safety	1%	3%	21%	—	1%
	Comparison	6%	12%	100%	—	6%
	Food Safety	3%	0%	0%	100%	2%

Note: Some cells are suppressed to protect confidentiality. Sample sizes are rounded to conform to US Census Bureau disclosure protection rules.

Census Bureau data on employment and earnings. A major advantage of these data, as noted earlier, is that it is now possible to put the labor market outcomes of food safety researchers in the context of both other researchers and other workers in the same industries.

In comparing overall employment outcomes one year after separating from their university, food safety researchers were less likely to be employed relative to the overall analytical sample of nonfood safety

Table 8.2 *Labor Market Outcomes of Analytical Sample*

	Analytical Sample				
		On Award with Text Analysis			
	All	Nonfood Safety	Comparison	Food Safety	Doctoral Recipients
Sample Size	9,400	5,000	600	250	4,000
		Earnings One Year after Exiting			
Annual Earnings	$60,565	$57,968	$46,162	$46,120	$63,172
Relative to Industry Sector	1.75	1.69	1.37	1.31	1.84
		Employment			
Employed	58%	59%	53%	53%	64%
Select Sectors	34%	36%	38%	34%	38%
Nonprofit	D	0%	N/A	N/A	0%
Government	6%	6%	5%	7%	7%
Food Safety	D	1%	2%	N/A	1%
Academia	27%	29%	32%	26%	31%
		Earnings One Year after Exiting			
Annual Earnings	$60,565	$57,968	$46,162	$46,120	$63,172
Relative to Industry Sector	1.75	1.69	1.37	1.31	1.84

Note: Some cells are suppressed (D) to protect confidentiality. Sample sizes are rounded to conform to Census Bureau disclosure protection rules.

researchers but about as likely as those in the comparison group. Similarly, postseparation earnings and industry-relative earnings of food safety researchers were low relative to the overall analytical sample but very close to those in the comparison group. Employment for food safety researchers was lower relative to both groups in the aggregate of the academic, government, nonprofit, and food safety industry sectors. Within that group of select sectors, food safety researchers were slightly more likely, in percentage point terms, to find employment in the government sector but far less likely to be employed in academia. One straightforward explanation of this disparity might be that food safety researchers were more likely to have been enrolled in non-PhD-granting graduate programs or less likely to complete a program in their terminal degree. However, the study found and subsequently reported evidence that suggests the reverse is true for food safety researchers relative to the overall analytical sample.

Earnings for graduate students and postdoctoral researchers in food safety research are substantially less than for their counterparts in other research fields. They earn about $46,000 a year; their counterparts earn about $60,000 a year. However, as mentioned earlier, the other research fields for comparison include computer science, finance, and engineering – and researchers in those fields have different skill sets and operate in different labor markets. When the food safety researcher earnings are compared with a more comparable group, the earnings are very similar.

Interestingly, the same pattern holds when earnings are compared with earnings in the industry of employment. The match to US Census Bureau data enables the comparison of earnings of the researchers with the earnings of other workers in their industry. Research-trained individuals one year after leaving the university earn, on average, about 75 percent more than their coworkers in that industry. However, both food safety researchers and researchers in their comparison group make between 30 and 37 percent more than others in that industry.

8.5 Analytical Results

Section 8.4 provided simple descriptive statistics on the differences in labor market outcomes for food safety researchers relative to other groups in the economy. This section uses multivariate regressions to summarize the differences while controlling for a variety of confounding factors, such as demographic characteristics and the date of separation.

8.5.1 Employment Differences

This subsection examines the employment outcomes of food safety researchers subsequent to their leaving the research institution. The focus is first on whether they got a job in the United States. Next, other sector-specific employment outcomes were examined, such as jobs in academia, government, nonprofit, or food safety industry sectors.

Table 8.3 presents estimates from a logistic regression of employment in these select sectors on the food safety research indicator, as well as controls. As before, each panel gradually restricts the empirical sample, and the table presents exponentiated coefficient estimates. Relative to the overall analytical sample, food safety researchers were nearly twice as likely to be employed in these select industries. However, this difference did not persist through the more restrictive samples shown in the second and third panels. Note that the coefficient estimates are consistently of the same

Table 8.3 *Logistic Regression of Sector-Specific Employment on Food Safety Funding and Controls*

Dependent Variable: Employed All Food Safety Industries	Analytical Sample						Comparison Grants		
	All			NSF, NIH, and USDA grants					
	(1)	(2)	(3)	(4)	(5)	(6)	(7)	(8)	(9)
Food Safety Research	1.78**	1.70**	1.86*	1.14	1.19	1.27	1.54	1.16	1.16
	(0.40)	(0.45)	(0.67)	(0.39)	(0.33)	(0.32)	(1.56)	(1.25)	(1.21)
Agency	X	X	X	X	X	X	X	X	X
Occupation	X	X	X	X	X	X	X	X	X
University	X	X	X	X	X	X	X	X	X
Cohort	X	X	X	X	X	X	X	X	X
Demographics		X	X		X	X		X	X
Award Length			X			X			X
Pseudo R^2	0.0242	0.0448	0.0489	0.0394	0.0619	0.0638	0.0828	0.1048	0.1058
Sample Size	5,100	5,100	5,100	3,000	3,000	3,000	450	450	450

Note: Coefficients are presented as odds-ratios and are concatenated, with ** indicating significance at the 5 percent level and * indicating significance at the 10 percent level. Standard errors are contained in parentheses where they have been clustered at the university level. All regressions include controls for agency (e.g., dummies for not food safety NIH, NSF, or USDA awards), cohort (e.g., year of exit), university, occupation (graduate student or postdoc), demographics, and the length an individual is on an award. The sample is restricted to individuals matched to the LEHD Individual Characteristics File (ICF) where demographic controls include age, age squared, sex, race (white, black, Asian, and all other), Hispanic/non-Hispanic, place of birth (United States, Asia, Western Europe and Canada, and all other). Controls included in each specification are indicated with an "X." The results are robust to clustering at the cohort level as well as correcting for selection into the LEHD ICF using a Heckman correction or inverse propensity score weighting.

137

sign and magnitude across specifications but are insignificant, possibly due to a lack of statistical power from this small portion of the analytical sample.

8.5.2 Earnings Outcomes

Table 8.3 reports the results from regressing the log of annualized earnings one year after separation from grant funding on a dichotomous indicator of food safety support and a series of controls. In the leftmost panel, the estimation sample includes all individuals on food safety awards as well as any individual in our analytical sample.

The middle panel reports earnings relative to the sample of researchers on awards processed using text analysis that includes food safety awards and nonfood safety awards made by NIH, NSF, and USDA. The rightmost panel includes only food safety researchers as well as the main comparison group consisting of researchers on awards issued by food safety–intensive programs and the USDA. Across the specifications within each panel, a more restrictive set of controls is gradually introduced that includes flags for agency support, occupation (e.g., graduate student or postdoc), cohort (e.g., separation year), university, demographics, and overall time spent in the last 24 months on all grant-funded activity. Relative to the overall analytical sample and subset of researchers on awards with text analysis, the food safety researchers were observed to earn between 24 and 48 percent less. However, this earnings deficit does not persist through our estimates relative to the comparison group of similar awards.

As an alternative to the previous estimation relying on log earnings, earnings were instead normalized by industry sector by using the mean earnings across UMETRICS individuals regardless of whether they met our definition for the analytical sample. Although different in terms of mechanics, this specification is comparable to one where industry indicator variables might be added, in that it allows us to control for employment in industries with disproportionally low earnings. In examining the results from Table 8.5 and comparing those coefficient estimates with those obtained in Table 8.4, the earnings disparity for food safety researchers relative to the overall analytical sample persists. Note again that the rightmost panel, where the comparison is restricted to those individuals funded by USDA awards and food safety intensive programs, is statistically insignificant, but the coefficient estimates suggest a true estimate that approaches zero.

Table 8.4 *Linear Regression of Log Earnings on Food Safety Funding and Controls*

Dependent Variable: log(Earnings)	All Individuals			NSF, NIH, and USDA Grants			Comparison Grants		
	(1)	(2)	(3)	(4)	(5)	(6)	(7)	(8)	(9)
Food Safety	-0.48***	-0.43***	-0.45***	-0.28	-0.24*	-0.27*	0.10	-0.05	-0.05
	(0.11)	(0.09)	(0.09)	(0.20)	(0.14)	(0.14)	(0.27)	(0.24)	(0.25)
Agency	X	X	X	X	X	X	X	X	X
Occupation	X	X	X	X	X	X	X	X	X
Cohort	X	X	X	X	X	X	X	X	X
University	X	X	X	X	X	X	X	X	X
Demographics		X	X		X	X		X	X
Award Length			X			X			X
Pseudo R^2	0.2100	0.2220	0.2290	0.2100	0.2330	0.2350	0.3280	0.3370	0.3540
Sample Size	5,100	5,100	5,100	3,000	3,000	3,000	450	450	450

Note: Coefficients are concatenated with *** indicating significance at the 1 percent level and * indicating significance at the 10 percent level. Standard errors are contained in parentheses where they have been clustered at the university level. All regressions include controls for agency (e.g., dummies for not food safety NIH, NSF, or USDA awards), cohort (e.g., year of exit), university, occupation (graduate student or postdoc), demographics, and the length an individual is on an award. The sample is restricted to individuals matched to the LEHD ICF file where demographic controls include age, age squared, sex, race (white, black, Asian, and all other), Hispanic/non-Hispanic, place of birth (United States, Asia, Western Europe and Canada, and all other). Controls included in each specification indicated with X. The results are robust to clustering at the cohort level as well as correcting for selection into the LEHD ICF using a Heckman correction or inverse propensity score weighting.

Table 8.5 *Linear Regression of One Year Relative Log Wages on Food Safety Funding and Controls*

	Analytical Sample						Comparison Grants		
	All			NSF, NIH, and USDA Grants					
Dependent Variable: Relative Wage + 1 year	(1)	(2)	(3)	(4)	(5)	(6)	(7)	(8)	(9)
Food Safety	-0.54***	-0.50***	-0.50***	-0.36**	-0.33**	-0.34**	0.03	0.00	-0.01
	(0.12)	(0.11)	(0.11)	(0.17)	(0.16)	(0.16)	(0.21)	(0.20)	(0.20)
Agency	X	X	X	X	X	X	X	X	X
Occupation	X	X	X	X	X	X	X	X	X
University	X	X	X	X	X	X	X	X	X
Cohort	X	X	X	X	X	X	X	X	X
Demographics		X	X		X	X		X	X
Award Length			X			X			X
Pseudo R^2	0.0740	0.0880	0.0900	0.0710	0.1110	0.1120	0.1580	0.1730	0.1840
Sample Size	5,100	5,100	5,100	3,000	3,000	3,000	450	450	450

Note: Coefficients are concatenated with *** indicating significance at the 1 percent level and ** indicating significance at the 5 percent level. Standard errors are contained in parentheses where they have been clustered at the university level. All regressions include controls for agency (e.g., dummies for not food safety NIH, NSF, or USDA awards), cohort (e.g., year of exit), university, occupation (graduate student or postdoc), demographics, and the length an individual is on an award. The sample is restricted to individuals matched to the LEHD ICF file where demographic controls include age, age squared, sex, race (white, black, Asian, and all other), Hispanic/non-Hispanic, place of birth (United States, Asia, Western Europe and Canada, and all other). Controls included in each specification indicated with X. The results are robust to clustering at the cohort level as well as correcting for selection into the LEHD ICF using a Heckman correction or inverse propensity score weighting.

It is perhaps meaningful that regression results with earnings relative to industry sector as the dependent variable returned larger, more statistically significant coefficient estimates than regressions with earnings relative to dollar wages. High or low earnings outliers for some individuals are a possible explanation. However, this approach estimates a separate effect for employment industry or sector, so employment of food safety researchers in lower-paying sectors cannot explain lower earnings. Another possibility is that researchers connected with food safety awards obtain jobs more closely connected to agricultural production in rural locations or in other locations with generally lower wages. Even if true, this possibility does not appear to change the overall negative effects on earnings for food safety research or the pattern of estimates for the other covariates.

8.6 Dissertation Outcomes

The study's analysis of dissertation outcomes of early career researchers includes all the graduate students and postdoctoral researchers in the analytical sample. The binary outcome was modeled of whether an individual is matched with a dissertation in the ProQuest database using a logistic regression. Of the 9,400 individuals in our analytical sample, approximately 4,000 were matched to ProQuest. For this analysis, it was assumed that individuals who were not matched, including those who were not pursuing a doctoral degree, did not complete a dissertation. Table 8.6 reports the results of applying an indicator of earning a dissertation on the food safety indicator and controls. As before, evidence was found suggesting that food safety researchers were more likely to earn a PhD relative to the full text analysis sample.

8.7 Summary

This chapter explored the outcomes of early career researchers who participated in federally funded research awards as part of their training. Controlling for individual characteristics, including race and gender, participants in food safety research had lower earnings relative to the entire analytical sample of early career researchers. That differential disappeared when compared with researchers in closely related comparison groups developed from funding programs observed in the UMETRICS data.

Food safety researchers are more likely than other researchers to find employment in government, but the study controlled for sector of

Table 8.6 *Logistic Regression of PhD Achievement on Food Safety Funding and Controls*

	Analytical Sample								
	All			NSF, NIH, and USDA Grants			Comparison Grants		
Dependent Variable: PhD Earned	(1)	(2)	(3)	(4)	(5)	(6)	(7)	(8)	(9)
Food Safety	0.88	0.69	0.69	1.40*	1.69***	1.61***	2.14	1.06	0.68
	(0.27)	(0.42)	(0.42)	(0.24)	(0.34)	(0.27)	(2.01)	(0.77)	(0.30)
Agency	X	X	X	X	X	X	X	X	X
Occupation	X	X	X	X	X	X	X	X	X
University	X	X	X	X	X	X	X	X	X
Cohort	X	X	X	X	X	X	X	X	X
Demographics		X	X		X	X		X	X
Award Length			X			X			X
Pseudo R²	0.2503	0.3042	0.3042	0.2897	0.3273	0.3277	0.4274	0.5273	0.5446
Sample Size	4,000	4,000	4,000	2,320	2,320	2,320	320	320	320

Note: Coefficients are presented as odds-ratios and are concatenated with *** indicating significance at the 1 percent level and * indicating significance at the 10 percent level. Standard errors are contained in parentheses where they have been clustered at the university level. All regressions include controls for agency (e.g., dummies for not food safety NIH, NSF, or USDA awards), cohort (e.g., year of exit), university, occupation (graduate student or postdoc), demographics, and the length an individual is on an award. The sample is restricted to individuals matched to the LEHD ICF file where demographic controls include age, age squared, sex, race (white, black, Asian, and all other), Hispanic/non-Hispanic, place of birth (United States, Asia, Western Europe and Canada, and all other). Controls included in each specification indicated with X. The results are robust to clustering at the cohort level as well as correcting for selection into the LEHD ICF using a Heckman correction or inverse propensity score weighting.

142

employment, so that fact alone does not explain the lower wages of food safety researcher participants. Lower wages could be explained by a greater proportion of food safety graduate students who pursue master's degrees rather than doctoral degrees. This is also consistent with overall patterns of research funding and dissertation authorship, but not something the study observed directly about the graduate students in the sample. Dietz and Bozeman do not find evidence that experience as a graduate student researcher enhances subsequent research productivity in terms of patents or publications, but this lack of finding does not explain lower earnings for food safety researchers relative to other graduate researchers in different fields (*21*). A more likely explanation is that the market externalities that result in lower private investment in food safety also extend to labor market signals for early career food safety scientists. All else equal, providing research funding to early career scientists during their training might be insufficient to persuade them to devote the time to acquiring expertise specific to food safety if the posttraining job markets will not support them (*7, 8*). The relatively high employment rate of early career food safety researchers in government adds supporting evidence to this interpretation, highlighting the significance of the public sector in food safety.

The study also observed lower rates of employment for food safety researchers. This is most likely due to lower absorption of foreign-born food safety researchers into the US workforce. As with early career researchers in nonfood safety fields, employment in academia is a likely employment outcome. Future research could investigate how often these researchers continue to research food safety topics (and how often researchers from other disciplines take up food safety topics).

References

[1] N. Zolas et al., Wrapping It Up in a Person: Tracing Flows from Funded Research into the Economy. *Science* **350**, 1367–1371 (2015).

[2] Z. Griliches, Hybrid Corn: An Exploration in the Economics of Technological Change. *Econometrica* **25** (4), 501–522 (1957).

[3] W. E. Huffman, R. E. Evenson, *Science for Agriculture: A Long-Term Perspective* (John Wiley & Sons, 2008).

[4] V. E. Ball, J.-C. Bureau, J.-P. Butault, R. Nehring, Levels of Farm Sector Productivity: An International Comparison. *J. Product. Anal.* **15**, 5–29 (2001).

[5] J. Fernandez-Cornejo et al., "Pesticide Use in U.S. Agriculture: 21 Selected Crops, 1960–2008" (Economic Research Service US Department of Agriculture, Washington, DC, 2014), available at www.ers.usda.gov/webdocs/publications/43854/46734_eib124.pdf?v=41830

[6] V. E. Ball, C. A. K. Lovell, H. Luu, R. Nehring, Incorporating Environmental Impacts in the Measurement of Agricultural Productivity Growth. *J. Agric. Resour. Econ.*, 436–460 (2004).

[7] USDA Office of the Chief Scientist, "Food Safety Science White Paper" (2012), available at www.usda.gov/sites/default/files/documents/food-safety-science-white-paper.pdf.

[8] K. Fuglie et al., "Research Investments and Market Structure in the Food Processing, Agricultural Input, and Biofuel Industries Worldwide" (Economic Research Service US Department of Agriculture, Washington, DC, 2011).

[9] B. N. Sampat., appendix D in *Measuring the Impacts of Federal Investments in Research: A Workshop Summary*, National Research Council (National Academies Press, Washington, DC, 2011).

[10] R. B. Freeman, Data! Data! My Kingdom for Data! Data Needs for Analyzing the S&E Job Market. *Support RAND*, **32** (2004).

[11] J. Lane, S. Bertuzzi, Measuring the Results of Science Investments. *Science (80-.)* **331**, 678–680 (2010).

[12] F. Waldinger, Quality Matters: The Expulsion of Professors and the Consequences for PhD Students Outcomes in Nazi Germany. *J. Polit. Econ.*, 787–831 (2010).

[13] F. Waldinger, Peer Effects in Science: Evidence from the Dismissal of Scientists in Nazi Germany. *Rev. Econ. Stud.* **79**, 838–861 (2012).

[14] P. Stephan, in *Innovation Policy and the Economy*, vol. 7, J. Lerner, S. Stern, eds. (MIT Press, 2007).

[15] P. E. Stephan, *How Economics Shapes Science* (Harvard University Press, Cambridge, MA, 2012).

[16] R. Freeman, J. Van Reenen, in *Innovation Policy and the Economy*, vol. 9 (University of Chicago Press, 2009), pp. 1–38.

[17] J. Lane, J. Owen-Smith, R. F. Rosen, B. A. Weinberg, New Linked Data on Research Investments: Scientific Workforce, Productivity, and Public Value, *Res. Policy* **44**, 1659–1671 (2015).

[18] C. Buffington, B. C. Harris, C. Jones, B. A. Weinberg, STEM Training and Early Career Outcomes of Female and Male Graduate Students: Evidence from UMETRICS Data linked to the 2010 Census. *Am. Econ. Rev.* **106**, 333–338 (2016).

[19] M. Pezzoni, J. Mairesse, P. Stephan, J. Lane, Gender and the Publication Output of Graduate Students: A Case Study. *PLoS One* **11**, e0145146 (2016).

[20] M. Finn, "Stay Rates of Foreign Doctorate Recipients from US Universities, 2009" (Oak Ridge, TN, 2012).

[21] J. S. Dietz, B. Bozeman, Academic Careers, Patents, and Productivity: Industry Experience as Scientific and Technical Human Capital. *Res. Policy* **34**, 349–367 (2005).

9

Describing Patent Activity

Yeong Jae Kim, Evgeny Klochikhin, and Kaye Husbands Fealing

9.1 Overview

This chapter discusses how patent data can be used to provide additional information about the structure and commercialization of food safety research.[1] Although, historically, a great deal of the research evaluating the impact of science has relied on the study of patents (*1, 2*), this is not the case in food safety. Experts participating in the workshop entitled "Assessing the Public Value of Government-Funded University-Based Research on Food Safety," described in Chapter 2, pointed out that patents are not the primary output of food safety research and development; hence the goals of this chapter are limited to addressing the following questions: (1) What has happened to the pace and direction of patenting in the food safety sector? (2) What are the characteristics of US and foreign firms that are most active in food safety patenting? (3) What are the geographical and sectoral distribution of food safety patents?

This chapter provides new ways of answering these questions for two reasons. The first is the use of a new data set from the US Patent and Trademark Office (USPTO) that provides detailed information about patents, inventors, and firms. The second is the application of the text analysis techniques discussed in Chapter 4 to patent data – these techniques permit the identification of food safety patents in the same way that food safety awards were identified in earlier chapters.

---

[1] This chapter, and the one following, differ from Chapters 3–8 in that the approach is simply to describe food safety patenting writ large and is not the result of studying patenting activity of researchers who are funded in food safety.

9.2 Background

Although patents are widely used as a measure of innovation, they are not a perfect indicator for a number of reasons. All innovations are not necessarily patented, and patents do not necessarily lead to the commercialization of a product or process. There are variations in the propensity to patent across firms and sectors due to different market sizes and examination processes. A company could be strategically reluctant to file patent applications because it wants to hide its activities from its competitors. Once the technology has matured enough to dominate its competitors, the company may at that point file patent applications.

Given that the food safety industry spans a wide variety of sectors, the importance of patents could also vary depending on a firm's need to protect itself against imitators. For example, Fanfani et al. showed that patents related to agriculture and food industries in Italy are only one aspect of food industry innovations (3). They asserted that one cannot overlook the role of innovations that are not patentable. For this reason, using only patent data to identify food safety firms could omit firms that rely more on trade secrets or other strategic practices.

9.3 Data

The USPTO PatentsView[2] database is used to identify food safety patents and to retrieve additional data about patent assignees, inventors, their locations, and patent classifications.[3]

One of the primary advantages of using PatentsView is that the platform embeds disambiguated inventor and assignee identities as well as their related locations (4). For example, the same John M. Smith might apply for two patents with and without the middle initial. If one were looking at exact matches, these two inventors would be considered different individuals, while in fact they reside in the same city, patent in the same technology area, work for the same company, and so on. The new inventor disambiguation algorithm, authored by the research team from the University of Massachusetts at Amherst and integrated into PatentsView in 2016, uses discriminative hierarchical co-reference as a new approach to

---

[2]   www.patentsview.org/.
[3]   PatentsView is a collaborative initiative between the USPTO, the American Institutes for Research, New York University, the University of California at Berkeley, and two private software companies – Twin Arch Technologies and Periscopic

increase the quality of inventor disambiguation (5). The current assignee disambiguation uses the Jaro-Winkler approach by comparing string distance between patent assignee names and clustering similar organizations together (e.g., Google Inc. and Google should be considered as one entity). For locations, city/state/country text as it appears on the front of the patent is algorithmically matched to a master geocode file from Google and MaxMind open-source files.

Patent data contain highly technical legal language. As such, legal documents are hard to analyze with automated computational techniques because their syntactic and lexical structure differs significantly from narrative language (6). The authors of this chapter used a combination of both text analysis and patent classifications to identify food safety patents.

The text analysis approach that the study applied was to use expert-curated search terms to retrieve an initial set of potentially relevant patents and then manual review to determine the most appropriate classification. Such a keyword searches to find relevant patents and innovation descriptions are commonly used (e.g., see Shapira et al. (7), who used the search-based method to discern green industries focusing on green goods manufacturing). In this case, the study applied the keywords used in searching food safety research based on text analysis techniques referenced in Chapter 4. Patent titles and abstracts were extracted from the PatentsView database,[4] and then the search term strategy was applied, per Chapter 4. The initial set of potentially relevant patents for food safety contained 1,543 documents retrieved using the search term strategy. Clerical review showed that only a portion of these patents are truly related to food safety. Take, for example, patents US4008383 "Microwave oven door assembly" or US4034890 "Bread box," which were retrieved because a bread box is an example of a food safe (having same stem as "safety").

The second step was to use patent classifications to further specify the search criteria to retrieve only most relevant patents. For example, the patents mentioned in the preceding paragraph are classified as "Electric heating; electric lighting not otherwise provided for" and "Kitchen equipment; coffee mills; spice mills; apparatus for making beverages" by the Cooperative Patent Classification (CPC) and as "Electrical machinery, apparatus, energy" and "Furniture, games" by the World Intellectual Property Organization's (WIPO's) technology fields, respectively. Further

---

[4] Data as of July 15, 2016.

Table 9.1 *Categories of Food Safety Patents*

WIPO Field Titles	Frequency	Percent (%)
Food chemistry	2,204	51.3
Handling	709	16.5
Other special machines	325	7.57
Pharmaceuticals	241	5.61
Biotechnology	178	4.14
Basic materials chemistry	102	2.37
Organic fine chemistry	85	1.98
Medical technology	83	1.93
Surface technology, coating	69	1.61
Furniture, games	59	1.37
Others	241	5.62
Total	4,296	100

review showed that there is a link between CPC classes of individual patents and their relevance to food safety.

Two researchers on the team manually reviewed all patents and related CPC classes to identify which technology fields were most likely to represent food safety–related patents among the initial set of retrieved documents. The classes were further divided into three categories: sure, maybe, and irrelevant. Between 1976 and 2016, there are 675 patents with CPC classes from the "sure" category.[5] Taking these patents as the initial validated dataset, the study retrieved forward (cited by) and backward (cited) US patent citations. Forward and backward citations amounted to 4,179 and 3,708 patents, respectively.

A similar clerical review was conducted on the citations dataset and identified that the "sure" CPC classes also retrieve the most relevant food safety patents. The resultant dataset includes 2,038 forward and 2,030 backward citations. Given that some of these patents overlap, removing the duplicates resulted in the final set of 4,296 food safety patents that were used for further analysis.

Table 9.1 shows the number of food safety patents by WIPO technology fields. Patents related to food chemistry make up about half of all patents, because most technological innovations to improve food safety are related to the development of technologies that control and eliminate foodborne pathogens. An analysis of the CPCs reveals that food preparation or treatment is the top-ranked classification, followed by food storage and transport.

---

[5]   These were CPC classes A21, A22, A23, B08, and B32.

The results seem to be robust, based on an analysis of inventors, organizations, and patent classes. In particular, it is likely that inventors have a persistent patent portfolio and tend to file applications in a particular set of patent fields over time. Therefore, the technology categories of food safety patents should be similar to technology categories of other patent applications filed by the same inventors across years. The analysis identified 6,595 unique inventors that had food safety patents granted between 1976 and 2016. These inventors had been granted a total of 48,807 US patents, of which 4,296 are food safety patents. Every inventor had an average of 27.1 patents. The correlation between food safety patents and all patents per inventor is 0.32. In other words, there is a statistically significant link between the number of food safety and non-food safety patents filed by same inventors within same CPC classes: every food safety patent is associated with 0.6 non-food safety patents by the same inventor in given CPC classes, controlling for year and CPC fixed effects ($N = 31,572$). These measures suggest that inventors indeed tend to have persistent patent portfolios and file patent applications in similar fields, which is supportive of the validity of food safety patents selection.

It is also likely that assignee organizations follow a persistent patenting strategy and the number of food safety patents is likely to be linked with the number of non-food safety patents within similar CPC classes over time. Data were retrieved on 1,707 unique assignee organizations associated with selected food safety patents. The data vary significantly by size and specialization, with a standard deviation of 168.1 and a mean of 22.8 patents per assignee per year. Such variability leads to a small correlation of 0.03 between the number of food safety and non-food safety patents per assignee over time. If considering only assignees with smaller portfolios below the mean (<23), the correlation goes up to 0.08, showing that specialization matters in smaller organizations with less patenting activity.

Further analysis shows that there is a statistically significant link between food safety patents and non-food safety patents granted to same assignees within same CPC classes: each food safety patent is associated with 2.32 non-food safety patents, controlling for year and CPC class fixed effects ($N = 184,608$). These results indicate that assignees had persistent patent portfolios, where food safety patents were linked to non-food safety patents in a significant way.

Finally, the total number of patents filed under the CPC classes from the "sure" category and under the prevalent WIPO "Food Chemistry" technology field correlates with the number of food safety patents in those fields filed in similar years. The correlation coefficient between all patents

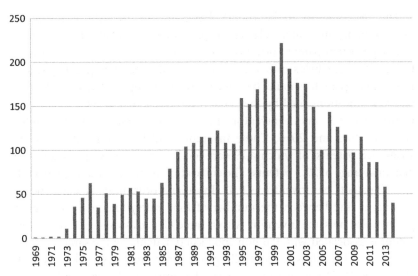

Figure 9.1 Food safety patent applications per year (1969–2015)

and food safety patents in these CPC classes is very high: 0.96. In the case of the Food Chemistry WIPO technology field, which represents the majority of identified food safety patents, the correlation between the number of food safety patents and all patents in this WIPO field is quite high, with the correlation coefficient of 0.85. Each food safety patent is associated with about 0.09 additional patents in this WIPO field. In essence, this means that almost all patents with the Food Chemistry WIPO field are related to food safety.

9.4 Analysis of Patenting Activity

Figure 9.1 shows the distribution of food safety patents by application year.[6] This distribution over time is rather uneven. These fluctuations may indicate the dependence of this technology sector on policies and market trends. For example, the 1993 *E. coli* outbreak was a turning point in food safety research. Several organizations, including the National Cattlemen's Beef Association, increased funding to conduct research on how to test and detect the pathogen effectively (8). Furthermore, the influx of food safety

---

[6] The analysis used application date rather than patent grant date, because of significant fluctuations in patent processing time in the years 1976–2016. On average, it has taken 2.6 years to grant a US patent after application since 1976.

research in the early 2000s coincided with the StarLink corn recall and significant public attention to the safety of genetically modified (GM) food. The European Union went as far as to ban all imports and planting of GM crops in 1998. The public concerns have dissipated since then, with science committees concluding that GM food is generally safe for human consumption, which consequently led to decreasing patenting activity in this topic.

In addition, several incentives and policy changes could have influenced the food safety patenting trends of past decades. Among others, Johnson stated that the Sanitary Food Transportation Act of 1990, the Nutrition Labeling and the Education Act of 1990 (NLEA), the Federal Tea Tasters Repeal Act of 1996, the Food Quality Protection Act of 1996, and the Public Health Security and Bioterrorism Preparedness and Response Act of 2002 could be among the policies that spurred food safety patenting activity as needing new technologies to address the challenges set forth by these laws (9).

9.4.1 Food Safety Firms

Table 9.2 shows the distribution of patent assignees by type. About 80 percent of assignees are US and foreign firms. The remaining organizations are universities, institutions, governments, hospitals, and individuals. While firms focus more on application of fundamental knowledge for commercial purposes, universities and institutes provide more fundamental research output. Governments are also a part of food safety research output, given that they are responsible for the protection of human health.

Table 9.2 *Food Safety Patent Assignees by Type*

Assignee Type	Frequency	Percent
US corporation	2,156	50.19
Foreign corporations, including state-owned	1,318	30.68
US individual	34	0.79
Foreign individual	14	0.33
US government	25	0.58
Foreign government	5	0.12
US state government	7	0.16
Undefined	736	17.13
Total	**4,296**	**100**

Figure 9.2 shows the geographic distribution of US companies and other entities with food safety patents. Most of these entities are concentrated in traditional innovation centers around New York and Boston, but many are scattered across the country, particularly in the Midwestern region, where agriculture is a major share of the local economy. Minneapolis–St. Paul, MN (127 patents); Cincinnati, OH (108); New York, NY (73); Northfield, IL (73); and Chicago, IL (46) are top five cities with most food safety patents.

The overwhelming majority of the US companies' patents are within the WIPO food chemistry technology field. Broader technology sectors covering food safety patents include chemistry, mechanical engineering, instruments, and electrical engineering. Patents across most of these categories are concentrated around New York, Minneapolis–St. Paul, and Cincinnati. However, patents related to electronic engineering and consumer electronics, such as microwaves and food refrigeration, are not as closely clustered and include places as far afield as Greeley, CO (15 patents); Kennesaw, GA (10); Wayzata, MN (4); New Port Richey, FL (4); and Wichita, KS (4).

Overall, US corporations face significant competition from large multinational companies based elsewhere. In particular, Swiss-based Nestec S.A. has the most food safety patents granted from 1976 to 2015. Tetra Laval Holdings & Finance S.A. is another Swiss company that is in the top 10 most patenting corporations. Together, large assignees that individually hold 15 or more food safety patents account for the majority of food safety–related patents and represent well-known food corporations (Table 9.3).

9.4.2 Federal Funding and Patent Activity

The link between food safety–related federal funding and economic outcomes is the primary topic of this book. Only a fraction of identified patents are directly associated with the federal government: 21 patents are assigned to the US Department of Agriculture (USDA), two are assigned to the US Secretary of the Army, and one is assigned to NASA.

Additionally, 37 patents have the so-called government interest statement that assigns full or partial interest in the given patent to the US government (Table 9.4). Some of these patents are co-funded by several government agencies. The USDA and affiliated institutions account for the bulk of these patents. The National Science Foundation (NSF) and National Institutes of Health have interest in four and nine food safety patents, respectively.

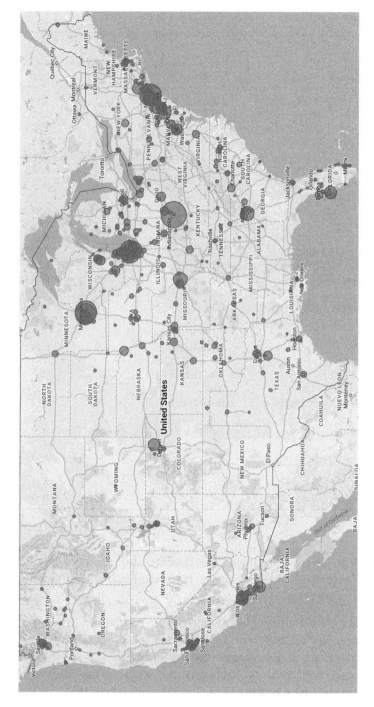

Figure 9.2 Geographic distribution of food safety companies and other entities with patents

Note: The node size reflects the relative number of patents assigned to firms situated in those locations.

Table 9.3 *Patent Applications by Parent Companies (1976–2015)*

Assignee Organization	Assignee Country	Assignee State/City	Number of Food Safety Patents	Share in Total
Nestec S.A.	Switzerland	Canton of Vaud	132	3.8
Procter & Gamble	USA	OH	88	2.53
Ecolab	USA	MN	47	1.35
Abbott Laboratories	USA	IL	33	0.95
Nabisco Brands	USA	NJ	33	0.95
Microlife Technics	USA	FL	32	0.92
Tetra Laval Holdings & Finance S.A.	Switzerland	VD	32	0.92
Coca-Cola	USA	GA	29	0.83
General Foods			22	0.63
Cargill	USA	MN	21	0.6
Kraft Foods	USA	IL	21	0.6
General Mills	USA	MN	20	0.58
Kraft Foods Global Brands	USA	IL	20	0.58
Kraft Foods Holdings	USA	IL	20	0.58
Medical Instill Technologies	USA	CT	20	0.58
Chr. Hansen A/S	Denmark	Hovedstaden, Capital Region of Denmark	19	0.55
Iams	USA	OH	19	0.55
Compagnie Gervais Danone	France	Ile-de-France	18	0.52
Kabushiki Kaisha Yakult Honsha	Japan	Tokyo	18	0.52
3form	USA	IL	17	0.49
Ajinomoto	Japan	Tokyo	15	0.43
AptarGroup	USA	IL	15	0.43
Paramount Packaging	USA	PA	15	0.43

Patents with government interest statements also mention specific awards and contracts, where available. For example, the NSF-funded patents refer to the following awards:

- NSF Alan T. Waterman Award (#9910949) to Chaitan Khosla for developing "an exciting new approach for the production of new antimicrobial agents from engineered organisms."
- Food Intake and Nutrition-Related Award studying the effect of a peptide in the brain, neuropeptide Y, on feeding (#9007573).

Table 9.4 *Government Interest Statements in Food Safety Patents*

Agency	Number of Patents
Army	3
Department of Agriculture	14
Department of Energy	3
National Institutes of Health	9
National Science Foundation	4
Centers for Disease Control and Prevention	1
US government (as a whole)	5
Total	39

- US-New Zealand Cooperative Research on Molecular Characterization and Modification of *Lactobacillus spp* (#9020678). The project studied the genetics, biology, and microbial ecology of lactobacilli, microorganisms that play an important role in the food fermentation industry and in animal husbandry.[7]

The majority of food safety patents with government interest are within the WIPO Food Chemistry, Pharmaceuticals, and Biotechnology fields.

9.5 Summary

The approach in this chapter can be seen as yielding a subset of food safety firms, mainly food producers and distributors, as well as packagers and producers. It is possible that some activity was missed in this chapter by the patent data. In particular, food service distributors that play an important role in providing food to restaurants and consumers may be missing from this analysis. The actual number of food safety firms could be much larger than the list of firms identified using the patent data. Perhaps most importantly, this chapter has provided guidance for those who use patent data to identify food safety firms in the future.

The scope of the firms can be subject to change depending on how one defines the boundaries for the firms. Since not all firms file patent applications, the scope of food safety firms in the patent data identified in this chapter is a lower bound. Using a more traditional method such as North

---

[7] Referred to by two patents US5922375 and US5902743, both of which were also cofunded by USDA AGRICCREE Grant No. 91-37201-6762 and HATCH #3360, and one of which was cofunded by an additional USDA Grant No. 92-38500-7110.

American Industrial Classification System (NAICS) codes by industry to identify food safety firms is likely to be misleading, because that process might omit newly emerging technology areas. This is in part because of the broad nature of the food safety industry, which encompasses food-related activities that range from farm to fork.

References

[1] B. N. Sampat, P. Azoulay, The Impact of Publicly Funded Biomedical and Health Research: A Review, in *Measuring the Impacts of Federal Investments in Research: A Workshop Summary*, National Research Council (Washington, DC: National Academies Press, 2011).

[2] P. Azoulay, J. S. G. Zivin, D. Li, B. N. Sampat, Public R&D Investments and Private-Sector Patenting: Evidence from NIH Funding Rules. *Natl. Bur. Econ. Res. Work. Pap. Ser.* **No. 20889** (2015), doi:10.3386/w20889.

[3] R. Fanfani, L. Lanini, S. Torroni, in *Economics of Innovation: The Case of Food Industry*, G. Galizzi, L. Venturini, eds. (Physica-Verlag HD, 1996), pp. 391–406.

[4] G.-C. Li et al., Disambiguation and Co-Authorship Networks of the U.S. Patent Inventor Database (1975–2010). *Res. Policy.* **43**, 941–955 (2014).

[5] M. Wick, S. Singh, A. Mccallum, A Discriminative Hierarchical Model for Fast Coreference at Large Scale. *ACL*, 379–388 (2012).

[6] R. Krestel, P. Smyth, Recommending Patents Based on Latent Topics. *Proc. 7th ACM Conf. Recomm. Syst. – RecSys '13*, 395–398 (2013).

[7] P. Shapira, A. Gök, E. Klochikhin, M. Sensier, Probing "Green" Industry Enterprises in the UK: A New Identification Approach. *Technol. Forecast. Soc. Change.* **85**, 93–104 (2014).

[8] E. Golan, T. Roberts, E. Salay, J. Caswell, M. Ollinger, D. Moore, *Food Safety Innovation in the United States: Evidence from the Meat Industry*, No. 34083 (United States Department of Agriculture, Economic Research Service, 2004).

[9] Johnson, R., Food Fraud and "Economically Motivated Adulteration" of Food and Food Ingredients. Congressional Research Service. CRS Report No. R43358 (2014).

10

Describing Scientific Outcomes

Evgeny Klochikhin and Kaye Husbands Fealing

10.1 Introduction

Academic publications play an increasing role in assessing the results of science funding and evaluating academic performance. National evaluation frameworks, such as the Research Excellence Framework in the United Kingdom,[1] assign much weight to publication outputs and journal ratings in their evaluation of individual institutions (and researchers). "Publish or Perish" is a phrase that is typically used to describe the increasing pressure on academia to publish rapidly and continually to sustain their careers (1). Bibliometrics and library science are the major disciplines looking at publications and producing citation and coauthor analysis to understand the value and level of scientific activities and collaborations (2).

Scientific papers are also important as a source of policy governance: agencies and legislatures look for evidence to guide their rule-making and legislative efforts. Food safety research can support the Food and Drug Administration (FDA), US Department of Agriculture (USDA), Centers for Disease Control and Prevention (CDC), and US Congress in setting food policy priorities and enforcing regulations where they are needed most.

This chapter looks at food safety–related publications, representative of this research. Using the method described in Chapter 4, information retrieval techniques were applied to conduct a systematic search of food safety documents across several databases and further analyze them from the perspective of funding acknowledgments and topical bias.

The chapter describes the landscape of food safety research and benchmarks these scientific outputs with the funding inputs described in Chapter 4. The method also seeks to address two major weaknesses of

[1] www.ref.ac.uk.

traditional bibliometric analysis: (1) limited coverage (and bias) of analyzed literature, due to the limitations of existing databases that tend to include a specific set of journals and subjects (interesting to their primary readership) and (2) the high cost of running a large-scale qualitative analysis of retrieved publications. New computational approaches can address both weaknesses in a scalable and replicable way.

10.2 Approach

Bibliometrics employs library science approaches that use search strings to retrieve relevant articles. The proliferation of academic journals, due to the development of digital content, has led to increasing number of scientific databases supported by publishers (e.g., Elsevier and Taylor & Francis), and large media companies (e.g., Thomson Reuters). Each database has a unique interface and query rules, which poses a question of consistency and reliability of results retrieved from all sources using the same search string.

Other challenges are also common when creating a reference set of articles for benchmarking and performance evaluation (3). The well-known Hirsch index and journal impact factor are biased toward highly cited scientific fields and publication outlets while underscoring research in specialized areas with a limited number of authors. For example, authors in physics are much more likely to have a high citation rate than those in economics or humanities.

Innovative social science and computational approaches can help address these limitations. Systematic literature reviews, originally from medical sciences and now increasingly used in impact evaluation and international development, seek to reduce the bias of traditional literature reviews by conducting document searches systematically and introducing additional statistical validation techniques (4). Computational approaches, such as the one described in Chapter 4, can be used to increase the scope and coverage of the systematic literature review (5) by including multiple databases and strict selection criteria to retrieve only relevant documents. The documents should first be retrieved from selected databases (e.g., Web of Science and ScienceDirect) stored in a controlled database environment (e.g., in a newly created relational database), and then reexamined using the standardized search strings and the wikilabeling approach. Running the searches in a controlled database environment ensures that only the documents satisfying all search criteria are retained for further analysis.

This study used the data retrieved from the Thomson Reuters Web of Science (WoS). The database contains publications from selected journals that are part of the Journal Citation Index, that is, peer-reviewed publications that are in good standing with the academic community as shown by the number of citations. The WoS is frequently used for bibliometric studies owing to its simple structure and a number of additional variables, such as the knowledge area for journals for (inter)disciplinary analysis (6).

Note, however, that different databases may have bias in content areas and coverage, especially with regard to publication languages and topics. For example, Rafols et al. demonstrated that the popular Scopus and WoS databases significantly underreport research relevant to local needs of low- and middle-income countries (7). Meanwhile, the database of the Centre for Agriculture and Biosciences International (CABI) provides better coverage of the research on rice relevant to the developing world.

To measure this bias, the data were retrieved from a number of other academic databases (Box 10.1). Given the limitations of selected databases, this project used only the first query string under the "general" category to retrieve data for this analysis (see Appendix 10.1 at the end of this chapter for the exact query string). In particular, the databases have a cap on the number of publication abstracts that can be exported for further analysis. For example, ScienceDirect allows viewing of only up to 2,000 results per query, which makes the process of retrieving the complete data set rather complicated. As such, all publication data from 2000 to 2016 were exported from selected databases, except for ScienceDirect, where coverage is limited to 2000–2010 due to export limitations. While acknowledging the limitations of this approach, the main purpose of retrieving these data was to measure the bias of food safety publication coverage in WoS versus other academic databases.

Box 10.1 List of Data Sources for This Approach

- SAGE Publications
- ScienceDirect
- Taylor & Francis
- Wiley
- Cochrane Library
- JSTOR Arts & Sciences Collections I through X and Business III
- Within EBSCO
  - Academic Search Premier
  - EconLit
  - Education Source
  - ERIC
  - Psychology and Behavioral Sciences Collection
  - PsycINFO
  - SocINDEX with Full Text

Our analysis was based on two premises: (1) analyzing the overlap and differences between food safety publications in Web of Sciences and all other databases and (2) inferring the topic model of food safety grants onto the WoS publication records to gain insights into how well publication activity was aligned with the federally funded research landscape. The latter analysis helped us better understand the relationship between science and policy, in terms of what is being funded and what the primary scientific focus is for the food safety research community.

10.3 Implementation

Schuelke-Leech et al. note that to maximize the coverage and completeness of collected data, such as scientific publications, the search strategy needs to be broad to retrieve as many potentially relevant items from all databases as possible (8). The first property – ability to search the full database – is critical to ensure impartiality of the selection process. For example, Google Scholar is a crucial source of various literature types, particularly gray literature and unpublished papers. However, it does not provide an interface that would allow us to search and retrieve all potentially relevant documents systematically. In other words, when running a query, should only the top 50 results be retrieved, or the top 100, top 200, or yet another number?

The search rules are not standardized across the different repositories. For example, the Thomson Reuters WoS instructs users to include search phrases in parentheses, for example, *(food safe*)*, while other sources, such as SAGE Publications, require phrases to be encapsulated in double quotation marks, for example, *"food safety"*. The rules of using Boolean logic, including wildcards (e.g., "*" and "?"), are also different across various sources. Furthermore, there are often limits on the number of queries and length of search strings.

The solution was to retrieve as many potentially relevant documents as possible from the selected databases. Once these documents were retrieved and stored in a local database along with text abstracts, one standardized search string was applied to all documents. The use of one standardized search string then ensured that an unbiased search strategy was followed, therefore ruling out any inconsistencies between varying data sources.

The stylized search string used for the publication retrieval process is the same as described in Chapter 4, with slight modifications for various databases (see Appendix 10.1). Wikilabeling was then applied to the retrieved documents to evaluate the entire context of the paper abstracts for relevance to food safety.

One last step of effective data collection relates to processing difficulties. As much as 90 percent of further analysis could depend on the quality and structure of the data processing approach (9). For the purpose of this project, the Mendeley software was used to store and organize retrieved literature references. The underlying relational database (SQLite) was then directly accessed for flexibility and validation purposes. The fields used for the approach, described in Section 10.4, include textual data and identification information, for instance, a unique identifier of every document, its title and abstract.

10.4 Results

This project used the stylized search strings to retrieve the initial document set from Thomson Reuters WoS with publication years between 2000 and mid-2016. The search returned 130,826 documents in the following categories:[2]

- General: 38,438 documents
- Food pathogens: 68,907 documents
- Food processing: 20,804 documents
- Biochemistry: 9,004 documents
- Foodborne illnesses: 43,081 documents
- Toxins: 36,320 documents.

The standardized search string and wikilabeling were then applied on the retrieved document titles and abstracts.[3] The search term approach confirmed that 88,594 documents were retrieved by using a standardized search string.[4] Wikilabeling further reduced this number to 41,493 documents by evaluating the entire context of document abstracts for relevance to food safety. Among these are 39,115 journal articles, 982 books, and 1,396 book series. Figure 10.1 shows distribution of these documents over time.[5]

---

[2]　Some articles can fall under more than one search category.
[3]　See Chapter 4 for more details on the approach.
[4]　"Standardized search string" means that the regular expressions can be applied in a controlled environment where it is known exactly what types of documents are retrieved and how. Unlike the third-party databases, such as Thomson Reuters WoS, the individual data exports can be queried directly with controlled rules and information retrieval mechanisms.
[5]　The pace of publication increase can be misleading; there can be multiple reasons including the natural increase of food safety publication output and expansion of the

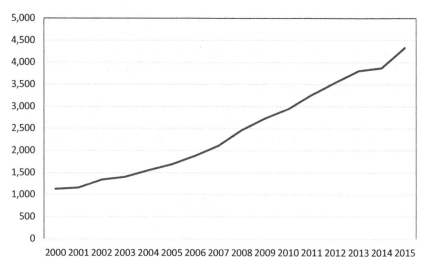

Figure 10.1 Number of WoS food safety publications (2000–2015)

Food safety journal articles retrieved from Thomson Reuters WoS were published in 3,877 journals. The overwhelming majority of articles were written in English (36,972 articles), with 615 published in German, 488 in French, 270 in Spanish, 220 in Portuguese, and 550 in other languages.

Table 10.1 shows the distribution of articles by research area. Food science and technology, microbiology, and biotechnology are top categories, covering about a third of all WoS food safety articles. There are, on average, 4.88 authors per food safety journal article retrieved from WoS. The majority of authors come from the United States, followed by China, Italy, France, and Spain (Table 10.2).

The majority of internationally coauthored papers are produced by collaborators based in the United States and in China, Canada, and England. English and Dutch researchers also collaborate often on food safety papers (Table 10.3). US researchers are authors on about 34 percent of all international WoS food safety papers. Intracountry US collaborators working in different institutions produced 3,081, or 7.8 percent, of all WoS food safety articles.

Overall, about 24.2 percent of WoS food safety papers involve cross-institutional collaboration. Intracountry US collaboration accounts for

WoS database itself to include more journals over time. Thomson Reuters tends to include all publications retrospectively in case a journal is added to the Journal Citation Index, but there still might be some inconsistencies in the process.

Table 10.1 *Top 15 Research Areas of Food Safety Journal Articles Retrieved from Thomson Reuters Web of Science*

Research Area	Number of WoS Journal Articles
Food Science and Technology	11,266
Microbiology	6,168
Biotechnology and Applied Microbiology	5,472
Immunology	4,051
Allergy	3,306
Agriculture	2,935
Chemistry	2,915
Veterinary Sciences	2,295
Environmental Sciences and Ecology	1,867
Toxicology	1,801
Biochemistry and Molecular Biology	1,650
Infectious Diseases	1,603
Nutrition and Dietetics	1,564
Public, Environmental, and Occupational Health	1,511
Pharmacology and Pharmacy	1,504

Table 10.2 *Top 10 Author Countries on Thomson Reuters Web of Science Food Safety Journal Articles*

Country	Number of Authors
USA	30,217
People's Republic of China	11,132
Italy	7,229
France	6,340
Spain	6,058
Germany	5,941
Japan	5,101
Brazil	5,036
England	4,746
South Korea	4,669

19 percent of all papers written solely by US-based authors, which suggests that food safety is concentrated in individual institutions and centers.

WoS also provides data related to funding acknowledgments mentioned on published papers. Among 39,115 food safety journal articles, about 40 percent of papers have a funding acknowledgments section. It is notable that only 1,858, or 12 percent, of these articles are written by authors working in 2 or more US institutions. In contrast, almost 30 percent of articles written

Table 10.3 *Top 10 International Food Safety Collaborators*

Country A	Country B	Number of Collaborative Articles
China	USA	368
Canada	USA	270
England	USA	241
England	Netherlands	194
Germany	USA	177
Australia	USA	161
Italy	England	160
England	Germany	158
Netherlands	USA	158
Italy	USA	157

by international collaborators have a funding acknowledgment section, with about 17 percent of such papers getting US government funding.

10.5 Analysis

The study first analyzed the potential coverage bias by comparing the publications data set retrieved from WoS and other databases. Next, the researchers reviewed the alignment between topic areas covered by the food safety publications and federally funded grants described in Chapter 4.

10.5.1 Topical Coverage

Searches were conducted on all of the databases in Box 10.1 using the "general" query string. The search returned 42,511 unique publication records. The researchers then applied the standardized search string and wikilabeling to identify only relevant documents. The final data set included 7,103 food safety publications: 6,599 journal articles, 61 news stories, 52 theses, 51 book chapters, and 340 others. Figure 10.2 shows steady growth of the number of food safety journal articles.

About 48 percent (3,167) of food safety publications were found in both WoS and other databases. To further understand the coverage bias, a topic model was run on the two datasets using the latent Dirichlet allocation algorithm (*10*).[6] Table 10.4 shows top 10 topics for both data sets.

---

[6] For valid comparison the project included only the WoS food safety articles that were retrieved by the "general" search string and dropped other records. Excluded were the

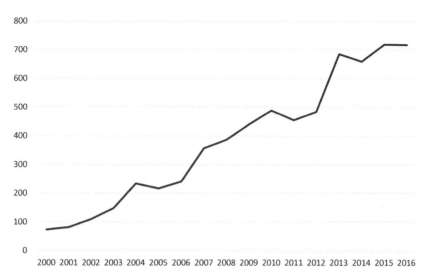

Figure 10.2 Number of food safety publications in various academic databases (2000–2016)

Interestingly, there are no vivid differences between the topic coverage of the two data sets. The interpretation can be twofold:

(1) Although WoS covers the most prestigious journals publishing food safety–related papers, these publications also represent the overall scientific landscape in this field, whereas authors publishing in journals not indexed by WoS follow the general trends.

(2) Both datasets primarily focus on regulatory and risk topics, including global food safety regulations, which suggests that topic is quite prominent and diverse in food safety research, which opens additional avenues for linking science to policy documents, such as Codex and FDA regulations. The lack of overlap in publications studying regulatory issues might also be explained by the fact that other databases (e.g., the Cochrane Library) might offer insights into linkages between funding in food safety science links and specific policies.

overlapping articles, so as to focus only on the differences between two publication sets. The resultant WoS data set included 6,371 records and the comparison data set had 3,936 publication abstracts.

Table 10.4 *Top 10 Topics for "General" Category of Food Safety Publications Retrieved from WoS and Other Databases*

WoS		Other databases	
Topic	Number of Publications (% of total)	Topic	Number of Publications (% of total)
regulatory global consumer producer framework governance certification challenge traceability china	630 (9.9)	outbreak fda salmonella discus contamination grower foodborne modernization illness focus	497 (12.6)
pathogen disease contamination foodborne food-borne bacterial surveillance veterinary emerging microorganism	443 (7.0)	consumer participant restaurant risk respondent handler behavior database perception foodborne	336 (8.5)
haccp microbial microbiological implementation hazard criterion monitoring fsms contamination predictive	387 (6.1)	regulatory global haccp risk challenge governance consumer codex microbiological implementation	254 (6.5)
consumer perception risk respondent attribute perceived strategy preference willingness purchasing	340 (5.3)	outbreak foodborne pathogen disease surveillance infection virus infectious parasite incidence	233 (5.9)
handler restaurant foodborne behavior vendor participant score establishment respondent significantly	337 (5.3)	residue efsa regulatory pesticide mrls framework reviewed mrl assessment rapporteur	229 (5.8)
detection assay dna biosensors bacteria pcr sensor antibody biosensor probe	286 (4.5)	detection pcr pathogen salmonella coli assay dna cfu spp bacteria	154 (3.9)
fishery global sustainable ecosystem farming aquaculture technology pest impact sustainability	252 (4.0)	bacteria microbial pathogen bacterial cfu coli microorganism contamination lactic lettuce	145 (3.7)

WoS		Other databases	
Topic	Number of Publications (% of total)	Topic	Number of Publications (% of total)
bacteria lactic packaging spore fermented lab treatment irradiation microbial microorganism	248 (3.9)	detection sensor assay antibody biosensors nanoparticles biosensor fluorescence immunoassay	143 (3.6)
spectroscopy spectrometry detection imaging fluorescence extraction chromatography raman melamine analytical	229 (3.6)	veterinary laboratory melamine trichinellosis pork review surveillance trichinella symptom veterinarian	125 (3.2)
salmonella poultry carcass pig pork campylobacter enteritidis broiler spp farm	224 (3.5)	mycotoxin aflatoxin contamination toxin metabolite afb1 fungal fungi ochratoxin fusarium	125 (3.2)

10.5.2 Topic Alignment between Publications and Federal Grants

Chapter 4 reports top topics identified in food safety awards funded by the USDA, National Science Foundation (NSF), and National Institutes of Health (NIH). The USDA grants cover the majority of all awards in the data set. Therefore, the researchers decided to use the topic model based on USDA grant data to identify how well these topics align with the publication landscape represented by the WoS food safety publication data.

The latent Dirichlet allocation algorithm allows inference of topics produced using one data set onto the other data set. Using this mechanism, the researchers studied whether the distribution of USDA grant topics was similar to research areas covered by WoS publications. As such, this analysis indicates how likely the USDA is to fund research that is most popular in the scientific community.

A more sophisticated analysis may be needed to include the time variable: For example, it is expected that papers coming out of grant research are likely to be published at least two years after the grant is funded. This assumption, however, does not hold when researchers use grants to promote their ongoing studies rather than to start a completely new research program.

Table 10.5 reports top 10 topics in USDA grant data and all WoS food safety publications. Some differences can be observed:

- Risk management and pathogen detection are among the common topics covered by both USDA grants and WoS food safety publications.
- USDA grants have a prominent topic focusing on consumer behavior and food safety in grocery stores. The topic is rather applied and does not seem to be covered substantially in WoS food safety publications (2.3 percent of publications are devoted to this topic).
- Similarly, the USDA funds workshop and education activities, which expectedly do not represent a substantial part of the publication data.
- At the same time, WoS publications cover several pathogen detection topics with practical applications. Further analysis may be needed to see whether these publications are more aligned with NSF-funded activities that include several grants in biotechnology, sensors, and pathogen detection (see Chapter 4).
- Noteworthy, USDA looks into the issues of waterborne pathogens, whereas WoS publications forego this topic (astonishingly, only 0.07 percent of WoS publications are devoted to this topic).
- WoS publications have food allergy as one of the more prominent topics. It might be that related activities are covered more substantially by NIH grants, which requires further investigation.

10.6 Summary

Food safety publications are important both as the knowledge outcomes of federally funded research and as a source of evidence for policymaking and regulation development. Advanced computational approaches, namely, standardized search strings and wikilabeling, help improve the validity, scope, and cost of bibliometric searches. Systematic literature reviews enhanced by meta-analysis can also serve as a tool for intervention planning and program evaluation, and to inform randomized controlled trials.

Using the technique described in Chapter 4, a set of 41,493 food safety documents was retrieved from the Thomson Reuters WoS, 39,115 of which are journal articles. About a quarter of these articles involve cross-institutional collaboration, and a third are in the fields of food science and technology, microbiology, and biotechnology. Funding acknowledgments are present on about 40 percent of food safety papers.

Table 10.5 *Top 10 Topics in USDA Grant Data and All WoS Food Safety Publications*

USDA		WoS	
Topic	Number of Grants (% of total)	Topic	Number of Publications (% of total)
pathogen contamination foodborne processor microbial haccp strategy intervention consumer hazard	120 (3.2)	bacteria probiotic gut intestinal microbiota lab lactobacillus culture gastrointestinal lactic	1,635 (6.7)
pathogen salmonella foodborne poultry food-borne outbreak contamination environment antimicrobial illness	107 (2.9)	monocytogenes listeria rte pathogen biofilm foodborne biofilms ready-to-eat contamination	1,144 (4.7)
foodborne consumer behavior foodservice educator evaluate implement illness grocery outreach	105 (2.8)	salmonella typhimurium enteritidis colonization salmonellosis enterica human poultry infection intestinal	1,021 (4.2)
waterborne pathogen disease niaid water-borne foodborne food protozoa	97 (2.6)	detection pathogen assay pcr detect diagnostic dna real-time bacterial detecting	973 (4.0)
fresh-cut processed microbial pathogen technology vegetable fruit treatment microorganism sensory	90 (2.4)	veterinary disease surveillance outbreak diagnostic veterinarian nahln emerging swine fmd	925 (3.8)
undergraduate sustainable nutrition usda lab experiential collaborative collaboration workshop curriculum	83 (2.2)	allergy allergen protein peptide soy allergic allergenicity allergenic epitope isoflavones	801 (3.3)
detection sensor biosensor pathogen toxin biosensors nanotechnology detect biological technology	81 (2.2)	detection sensor biosensor pathogen toxin biosensors nanotechnology detect biological technology	720 (3.0)

(*continued*)

Table 10.5 (*continued*)

USDA		WoS	
Topic	Number of Grants (% of total)	Topic	Number of Publications (% of total)
pathogen coli bacteria contamination salmonella bacterial microbial pathogenic foodborne	80 (2.1)	antioxidant nutritional dietary acid ingredient fatty extract lipid bioactive phenolic	710 (2.9)
mycotoxin contamination fungi fusarium toxin mycotoxigenic strategy graminearum fungal barley	75 (2.0)	mycotoxin contamination fungi fusarium toxin mycotoxigenic strategy graminearum fungal barley	702 (2.9)
antibiotic antimicrobial bacteria resistant bacterial pathogen pathogenic gene commensal farm	74 (2.0)	antibiotic antimicrobial bacteria resistant bacterial pathogen pathogenic gene commensal farm	650 (2.7)

While the analysis in this chapter does not directly link food safety research funding to publications through the UMETRICS database, there is evidence of common themes in USDA-funded research and WoS food safety publication. The main areas of overlap are risk management and pathogen detection. Activities downstream – closer to the fork than the farm in our original farm-to-fork schematic – are funded by the USDA, while publications are unsurprisingly focused on new knowledge and emerging techniques of detection and prevention. One exception to this finding is in the area of waterborne pathogens, where the USDA is making strong research investments; however, there is little apparent attention to this in the WoS literature. Going forward, greater insights into the efficacy of federal funding of food safety research on health outcomes through the publications pathway could be a fruitful avenue of exploration.

Appendix 10.1: Stylized Search Strings

The following are the search strings (by category) applied in various formats to extract information from the data sources.

1. General: ((food safety) OR (food securit*)) NOT ((hung*) OR (nutrit*) OR (calor*))

2. Food pathogens: ((food*) OR (dairy)) AND ((tetrodotoxin*) OR (myr-othecium*) OR (cyclopiazonic acid*) OR (fumitremorgen b*) OR (anisakis*) OR (coxiella burnetii*) OR (neurotoxic shellfish poisoning*) OR (eustrongylides*) OR (parasite*) OR (ergot alkaloids*) OR (yersinia pseudotuberculosis*) OR (zearalenone*) OR (taenia solium*) OR (pseudo-nitzschia pungens*) OR (phomopsins*) OR (shigella*) OR (campylobact*) OR (actinobacteria*) OR (lactic acid bacteria*) OR (grayanotoxin*) OR (acanthamoeba*) OR (nipah virus*) OR (arco-bacter butzleri*) OR (t-2 toxin*) OR (moniliformin*) OR (taenia saginata*) OR (verrucosidin*) OR (verruculogen*) OR (cryptosporid-ium parvum*) OR (aspergillus parasiticus*) OR (rotavirus*) OR (sal-monella*) OR (entamoeba histolytica*) OR (escherichia coli o157:h7*) OR (sterigmatocystin*) OR (fusarium*) OR (oosporeine*) OR (clostri-dium botulinum*) OR (fasciola hepatica*) OR (cryptosporidium*) OR (sporidesmin a*) OR (deoxynivalenol *) OR (listeria monocytogenes*) OR (3-nitropropionic acid*) OR (sarcocystis hominis*) OR (phytohae-magglutinin*) OR (brucella*) OR (protozoa*) OR (aspergillus flavus*) OR (trypanosoma cruzi*) OR (ergotamine*) OR (staphylococcus aur-eus*) OR (salmonellosis*) OR (fusarium moniliforme*) OR (clostri-dium perfringens*) OR (trichinella spiralis*) OR (nivalenol*) OR (3-nitropropionic acid*) OR (vibrio vulnificus*) OR (fusarochroma-none*) OR (toxoplasma gondii*) OR (fungus*) OR (paxilline*) OR (aflatoxins*) OR (cytochalasins*) OR (kojic acid*) OR (bacillus cer-eus*) OR (penitrem a*) OR (ciguatera poisoning*) OR (e. coli stec*) OR (fusaric acid*) OR (citreoviridin*) OR (cephalosporium*) OR (pyrrolizidine alkaloids*) OR (ddt*) OR (virulence properties of escher-ichia coli*) OR (cronobacter sakazakii*) OR (stachybotrys*) OR (tri-choderma*) OR (salmonella enteritidis*) OR (nanophyetus*) OR (enterovirus*) OR (lolitrem alkaloids*) OR (diphyllobothrium*) OR (scombrotoxin*) OR (zearalenols*) OR (aflatoxin*) OR (ascaris lum-bricoides*) OR (steroids*) OR (ochratoxins *) OR (norovirus*) OR (ht-2 toxin*) OR (listeria*) OR (sarcocystis*) OR (vibrio parahaemolyti-cus*) OR (yersinia enterocolitica*) OR (nematode*) OR (amnesic shellfish poisoning*) OR (giardia lamblia*) OR (aeromonas hydro-phila*) OR (ergopeptine alkaloids*) OR (fumonisins*) OR (staphylo-coccal enteritis*) OR (sarcocystis suihominis*) OR (patulin*) OR (diacetoxyscirpenol*) OR (corynebacterium ulcerans*) OR (pathogen*) OR (citrinin*) OR (streptococcus*) OR (anaerobic organism*) OR (alternaria*) OR (plesiomonas shigelloides*) OR (diarrhetic shellfish poisoning*) OR (caliciviridae*) OR (vibrio cholerae*) OR (cyclospora cayetanensis*) OR (astrovirus*) OR (platyhelminthes*))

3. Food processing: ((hygien*) OR (food safe*)) AND ((active packaging*) OR (animal feed*) OR (curing preserv*) OR (distribution*) OR (extrusion*) OR (industry*) OR (irradiation*) OR (manufacturing*) OR (packaging*) OR (preparation*) OR (preservation*) OR (processing*) OR (storage*) OR (technology*) OR (foodservice*) OR (freeze-drying*) OR (frozen food*) OR (good manufacturing practice*) OR (grocery stores*) OR (liquid packaging board*) OR (mandatory labelling*) OR (nutrasweet*) OR (package testing*) OR (packaging*) OR (packaging and labeling*) OR (pan frying*) OR (pasteurization*) OR (pickling*) OR (poaching cooking*) OR (preservative*) OR (pressure cooking*) OR (pressure frying*) OR (raw meat*) OR (refrigeration*) OR (searing*) OR (security seal*) OR (self-heating packaging*) OR (shallow frying*) OR (shrink wrap*) OR (slow cooker*) OR (smoking cooking*) OR (souring*) OR (steaming*) OR (stretch wrap*) OR (stuffing*) OR (tamper resistance*) OR (tamper-evident*) OR (tin can*) OR (ultra-high temperature processing*) OR (vacuum flask cooking*) OR (vacuum pack*))

4. Biochemistry: ((food*) AND (safe*)) AND (((acid-hydrolyzed vegetable protein*) OR (activated carbon*) OR (aquatic toxic*) OR (environmental microbio*) OR (environmental toxic*) OR (engineering*) OR (bioprocess tech*) OR (chemical toxi*) OR (biotechnology*) OR (chemistry*) OR (coloring*) OR (contaminant*) OR (dehydration*) OR (poisoning*) OR (forensic toxic*) OR (formaldehyde*) OR (lactic acid fermen*) OR (lactose*) OR (monosodium glut*) OR (mushroom poison*) OR (mycotoxin*) OR (paralytic shellfish poison*) OR (pesticide*) OR (pesticide residue*) OR (shellfish poisoning*) OR (sterilization microbio*) OR (succinate*) OR (sucralose*) OR (sugar subst*) OR (toxic capacity*) OR (toxicity class*) OR (toxin*) OR (traceab*) OR (transfat*) OR (trichothecenes*) OR (trichuris trichiura*)) OR (((foodbo?rne ill*) OR (foodbo?rne dis*)) AND (epidem*)) OR (((ill*) OR (disease) OR (hazard*)) AND ((genetically modified food*) OR (GM food) OR (genetic engin*))) OR (((allerg*) OR (sensitiv*)) AND (gluten*)))

5. Foodborne illnesses: ((food*) OR (foodbo?rn*) OR (food-rela*)) AND (((((ill*) OR (disease*)) AND (anemi*)) OR ((stomach flu*) OR (hepatitis a*) OR (hepatitis e*) OR (hygien*) OR (infection control*) OR (infectious dose*) OR (kidney failure*) OR (listeriosis*) OR (diarrhea*) OR (allergy*) OR (foodborne illness*) OR (gastroenteritis*)) OR (((safe*) OR (illness*) OR (disease*)) AND ((hand wash*) OR

(health hazard*) OR (toxic*) OR (health impact))) OR (((ETEC) OR (STEC) OR (coli)) AND ((health*) OR (hygien*) OR (vomit*))))

6. Toxins: (food*) AND ((safe*) OR (allerg*)) AND (((adulterated food*) OR (contaminated food*) OR (critical control point*) OR (danger zone safety*) OR (dietary suppl*) OR (european safety authority*) OR (fao*) OR (hygien*) OR (restaurant*) OR (fat substitute*) OR (federal food, drug, and cosmetic act*) OR (federal meat inspection act*) OR (fixed dose procedure*) OR (food safety act 1990*) OR (food standards agency*) OR (additive*) OR (hygien*) OR (labeling regulations*) OR (safe symbol*) OR (safety*) OR (food safety risk analys*) OR (sampling*) OR (diet* suppl*) OR (generally recognized as safe*) OR (grain quality*) OR (hazard analysis and critical control points*) OR (hazard analysis*) OR (iso 22000*) OR (iso 9000*) OR (infant formula*) OR (inspection*) OR (international association for protection*) OR (international safety network*) OR (nutrification*) OR (organic food*) OR (perishable food*) OR (potentially hazardous food*) OR (poultry products inspection act*) OR (quality assurance internation*) OR (rapid alert system for and feed*) OR (reference daily intake*) OR (starlink corn recall*) OR (title 21 of the code of federal regulations*) OR (total quality management*) OR (us and drug administration*)) OR ((foodbo?rn*) AND (pathogen*)) OR ((hazard*) AND (test* strip*)) OR ((hygien*) AND (regulat*)) OR (((fish) OR (seafood*)) AND (mercur*)) OR ((((ill*) OR (diseas*)) AND ((pcr test*) OR (oyster*) OR (sanita*))) OR ((pathogen* AND (source reduc*)))

References

[1] S. Rawat, S. Meena, Publish or Perish: Where Are We Heading? *J. Res. Med. Sci.* **19**, 87–89 (2014).

[2] P. Schaer, Applied Informetrics for Digital Libraries: An Overview of Foundations, Problems and Current Approaches. *Hist. Soc. Res.* **38**, 267–281 (2013).

[3] L. Bornmann, W. Marx, How Good Is Research Really? *EMBO Rep.* **14**, 226–230 (2013).

[4] H. Waddington et al., How to Do a Good Systematic Review of Effects in International Development: A Tool Kit. *J. Dev. Eff.* **9342**, 37–41 (2012).

[5] E. Klochikhin, T. De Hoop, R. Stone, "Better Coverage for Systematic Reviews in International Development Using Novel Computational Approaches." Manuscript under review (2016).

[6] A. Porter, I. Rafols, Is Science Becoming More Interdisciplinary? Measuring and Mapping Six Research Fields Over Time. *Scientometrics* 719–745 (2009).

[7] I. Rafols, T. Ciarli, D. Chavarro, Under-reporting Research Relevant to Local Needs in the Global South: Database Biases in the Representation of Knowledge on Rice Ismael. *ISSI* (2015), doi:10.1371/journal.pone.0062395.

[8] B.-A. Schuelke-Leech, B. Barry, M. Muratori, B. J. Yurkovich, Big Data Issues and Opportunities for Electric Utilities. *Renew. Sustain. Energy Rev.* **52**, 937–947 (2015).

[9] W. E. Winkler, Record Linkage, in D. Pfeffermann, C.R. Rao, eds., *Sample Surveys: Design, Methods and Applications. Handbook of Statistics 29A*, D. Pfeffermann and C. R. Rao, eds., pp. 351–380 (Elsevier, 2009).

[10] D. M. Blei, A. Y. Ng, M. I. Jordan, Latent Dirichlet Allocation. *J. Mach. Learn. Res.* **3**, 993–1022 (2003).

11

Conclusion

Kaye Husbands Fealing, Julia I. Lane, John L. King, and
Stanley R. Johnson

11.1 Overview

The United States spends more money on research and has more Nobel
Laureates than any other country. It is the unquestioned global leader in
science. But even while other countries are spending more on research and
development (R&D), purse strings are tightening in the United States, and
taxpayers want to know that their money is well spent.

But by and large, science investments are based on subjective decisions
and, often, flawed data (1). A major reason is that there is no systematic
answer to the very specific question of the link between federal R&D and
economic growth. As Ben Bernanke has pointed out, scholars do not know
much about how federal support for R&D affects economic activity (2).
The US government must and can do better: You cannot manage what you
cannot measure. As a House Science committee chair noted,

While many of us would agree that science has had a positive impact on our lives,
I think we actually know very little about how the process of innovation works.
What kinds of research programs or institutional structures are most effective?
How do investments in R&D translate to more jobs, improved health, and overall
societal wellbeing? How should we balance investments in basic and applied
research? With millions of Americans out of work, it becomes more critical than
ever that we find answers to these questions. (3)

Hitherto, the examination of the results of federal expenditures on scientific research has tried to directly link research grants to bibliometric
measures, like publications. This book argues that such an approach is
the wrong framework to use: Documents do not do science, people do
science. Science is not a slot machine wherein funding generates results in
nice tidy slices in three- to five-year time intervals. In fact, research ideas –
the black box between research funding and results – are transmitted

175

through networks in long, circuitous, and often nonlinear fashion, over quite long periods. So, the right framework begins with identifying the right unit of analysis – people – and examining how research funding builds public and private networks. The evidence is clear that people and networks are the drivers of innovation: The vibrant growth of Silicon Valley, Boston, San Diego, and the Research Triangle was driven by each region's research institutions and the people within them. Thorough analysis increasingly points to the importance of intangible flows of knowledge, such as contacts at conferences, business networking, and student flows from the bench to the workplace.

The approach taken in this book is to spell out a much more people-focused approach to describing (1) what research is being done, (2) who is doing the research, and (3) what the results are. The new granular data on principal investigators and their research teams (including students and postdoctoral researchers) – provide a trace of investments-to-outcomes and allow a rich narrative of how scientific investigators produce new ideas and human capital.

Focusing on food safety research, this book develops the data and techniques needed to generate trace measures from inputs to outcomes of the efficacy of federal expenditures in research, development, and innovation activities at 19 major research institutions. The project reported in this book enables better understanding of the "how" research-to-practice and research-to-commercialization processes, using both quantitative and qualitative evidence for the agricultural sector in general and food safety in particular. This study seeks to answer this question in three ways: by using new data, new technologies, and new methods.

Other key questions that this study addresses are: How do scientists themselves describe their research in food safety and security? How do these definitions vary across funding agencies? What expenditures have been made in food safety and security – not just by US Department of Agriculture (USDA) but by other federal agencies – and how have these expenditures changed over time? Who is doing research in food safety and security – including principal investigators, graduate students, postdoctoral researchers, and staff scientists? What are the research outputs at the university – journal articles, books, and patents – that are most relevant in the near and longer term to food safety in the United States? How are they linked to research funding?

A core feature of the project is the use of a multilayered, interconnected data platform – UMETRICS – which has granular information on all participants in all federally funded research projects for 19 major research universities, representing 30 percent of federal university-based R&D expenditures. Unique to these data are linkages between research grants from the National Science Foundation (NSF), the National Institutes of Health (NIH), and the USDA; patent data; longitudinal business data from the US Census Bureau; and ProQuest data on dissertations.

Innovative techniques used in this study include (1) using natural language processes to categorize fields of science, specifically a data taxonomy on food safety science; (2) showing the structure of food safety research funding with awards counts (size, duration) in different categories and at different agencies (NSF, NIH, and USDA); (3) showing new facts about the food safety research workforce, particularly focusing on research training at different institutions (by gender and age); (4) highlighting insights into research teams (training, jobs, research, team composition, and networks); (5) showing human capital outcomes related to placement and earnings (where are people placed, do they earn more with training under food safety grants, what are exit rates from the food safety field, and what are the firms/sectors where food safety students go after graduate school); (6) showing patent outcomes for foreign and domestic firms; (7) showing publication outcomes (including some foreign publications); and (8) providing earnings outcomes. These processes can be used to examine pathways to research the impact of federal funding in other domains.

Impact studies should frame outcomes for a given group relative to a comparison group. Merely stating that a given number or percentage of awards is granted does not convey the relevance of the finding. In this study, comparison groups allowed relative measures to be shown among the funders (NSF, NIH, and USDA) and among types of researchers examined (nonfood safety, food safety, and comparison groups).

11.2 What Have We Learned?

As stated in Chapter 1, "Introduction and Motivation," the research reported in this book is targeted at several categories of interest, including federal agencies that sponsor research, policymakers, university administrators, science and innovation policy researchers, and the general public. With that in mind, what follows are highlights of findings in Chapters 4 through 10.

Not surprisingly, Chapter 4 shows that the USDA has the highest intensity of food safety–related research awards compared with NSF and NIH. An estimated 6 percent of USDA awards fall in the food safety research and adjacent scientific fields.

A long-studied phenomenon of outputs from research funding is the concept of coproduction. In Chapter 5, connections between food safety grants and other funding sources were examined. On average, food safety awards were connected to roughly 22 other awards, while their comparison group peers were connected to 14 other awards. Furthermore, although there are clear ties to grantees funded by multiple agencies, such as the NSF, USDA, and NIH, the closest connection for food safety awards is to grants funded by NIH; the ties are less strong to awards that are funded by the NSF and USDA. This result highlights the point that research in any field builds on a broader research funding ecosystem, as well as the point that food safety research is particularly dependent on other research in the life sciences.

A critical component of this study is understanding the impact of funding on the development of human capital in food safety sectors. The analysis in Chapter 6 shows the following:

- With the benefit of linking the awards data to US Census data, employment and earnings outcomes were examined. A surprising finding was that, compared with their counterparts, food safety researchers who get jobs after graduate school were *less* likely to go to an academic job and *more* likely to take a government- or private-sector job.
- Male, US-born food safety researchers are *much more likely* to be employed than the other subgroups.
- Female US-born, male foreign-born, and female foreign-born food safety researchers are *much less likely* to be employed than the other subgroups.
- Earnings are lower for food safety researchers than for their counterparts, with earnings one year after leaving research funding averaging about $46,000, compared with $58,000 for all exiters. Composition effects might be the reason for this differential, given that there is a higher proportion of master's degree recipients (rather than PhDs) among the food safety exiters.
- Comparing the earnings of food safety researchers with those of all others in the sector in which they are employed. It is clear that research-trained workers earn substantially more than others in the sector, although the differential is smallest for food safety researchers.
- Foreign-born females in food safety research have similar earnings to their foreign-born counterparts, but are *much less likely* to be employed.

- US-born males in food safety research have higher employment rates, but lower earnings than their US-born male counterparts.
- Both US-born female and foreign-born male food safety researchers have lower employment rates and lower earnings than other researchers in the same demographic groups.

Looking at team size, Chapter 7 shows that teams composed of faculty, graduate students, and postdoctoral researcher have an average team size of roughly 27 food safety researchers. Food safety researchers work on larger teams than their counterparts.

Regression analysis allows for a richer analysis of the data discussed in Chapter 6. In Chapter 8, controlling for individual characteristics including race and gender, participants in food safety research still showed lower earnings relative to the entire analytical sample of early career researchers. However, that differential disappeared when comparing these data with researchers in more closely related comparison groups.

One of the traditional outputs measured, patents, are analyzed in Chapter 9. In this analysis, the focus is not on the number of patents generated, since food safety is more of a public than a private good. Here the focus is instead on using patents to identify firms that operate in food safety sectors.

- One outcome of this analysis is that inventors tend to have persistent patent portfolios and file patent applications in similar fields.
- Most entities are concentrated in traditional innovation centers around New York and Boston. Many are also scattered across the country, particularly in the midwestern region, where agriculture is a major share of the local economy.
- Large corporations that hold 15 or more food safety patents account for roughly 80 percent of all food safety–related patents.
- Most food safety patents with government interest are within the World Intellectual Property Organization (WIPO)'s food chemistry, pharmaceuticals, and biotechnology fields.

Chapter 10 looks at publications, another traditional area for impact studies. Although this study does not directly link funding to papers produced, it is possible to look at overlap between common themes. USDA-funded research and Web of Science (WoS) food safety publications similarly focus on risk management and pathogen detection. Activities downstream – closer to the fork than farm in our original farm-to-fork schematic – are funded by the USDA, while publications are unsurprisingly focused on new knowledge and emerging techniques of detection and prevention. One exception to this finding is in the area of waterborne pathogens, where the USDA is making strong investments in the science; however, there is little apparent attention to this in the WoS literature.

11.3 Extensions and Applications

As with any research agenda, much more can be done. Indeed, the data and the code have been made available through the Federal Statistical Research Data Centers and the Institute for Research on Innovation and Science (IRIS) so that the work here can be reproduced, extended, and improved. An illustrative, but not exhaustive, list would include the following.

A major area of interest should be the robustness of the text analysis. There are many different ways of classifying food safety – as the workshop participants pointed out. It is clear that there is no single best way to classify such a complex interdisciplinary field, and the results are likely to change with different sets of assumptions.

Another area of interest would be to delve into differences in the way in which food safety research is done in different institutions. How important is it to have an agricultural college or be located in a land grant institution? How important is it that there is a medical school?

As more data become available, it would be useful to study the labor market for food safety researchers. How do the career trajectories of food safety researchers evolve over time? How do market conditions affect how many junior researchers choose food safety as a research field? Are earnings relatively low because food safety researchers are not in great demand, or are there structural differences in the market? Do food safety researchers start up businesses as entrepreneurs?

11.4 Summary

The entire field of science of science policy was, in large part, initiated and fostered by John Marburger III. He remains the inspiration for much of the work reflected in this book. As he observed in a book published shortly before he died:

The inevitable absence of policy discipline in US federal government decision-making creates an imperative for some system of public education that fosters rational policy outcomes. The existence of an academic field of science of science policy is a necessary precondition for such a system. Policies can be formed and carried through rationally only when a sufficient number of men and women follow them in a deep, thoughtful, and open way. Science policy, in its broadest sense, has become so important that it deserves the enduring scrutiny from a profession of its own. This is the promise of the academic discipline of the science of science policy. (*4*)

The editors hope that the work in this book provides an initial set of steps that are based in a "deep, thoughtful, and open" framework. We very much hope that our work and this data infrastructure inspire a community of researchers to examine the pathways to research impact, in the manner described by Marburger.

References

[1] National Science and Technology Council, "The Science of Science Policy: A Federal Research Roadmap" (National Science and Technology Council, Science of Science Policy Interagency Task Group, Washington, DC, 2008).

[2] B. Bernanke, Promoting Research and Development: The Government's Role (2011), available at www.federalreserve.gov/newsevents/speech/bernanke2011 0516a.htm.

[3] D. Lipinski, *Opening Statement, House Science, Space, and Technology Committee, Hearing on the Science of Science and Innovation Policy, November 2, Rayburn Building, Washington, DC* (2010) (https://democrats-science.house.gov/legisla tion/hearings/science-science-and-innovation-policy).

[4] J. Marburger, in *The Handbook of Science of Science Policy*, K. H. Fealing, J. Lane, S. Shipp, eds. (Stanford University Press, 2011).

Index